CONFESSIONS OF
A MALE GYNECOLOGIST

A VIEW FROM THE OTHER SIDE OF THE STIRRUPS

ANDRE BELLANGER, M.D.

www.ConfessionsOfAMaleGynecologist.com

ISBN: 978-0692682364

Printed in the United States of America

First Printing 2016

Cover design:
JD&J Book Cover Design

Interior design:
Nand Kishore Pandey

Cover design photograph:
C'est Beau by Stephanie

"Thanks to Dr. Bellanger's knack for telling a story while teaching a lesson, reading *Confessions of a Male Gynecologist* was an entertaining experience. I cringed when I came to the chapter 'The Air Down There,' but I had to read every word. Finally, the unspeakable has been addressed. And, the author's purely medical opinion about abortion provides an insightful viewpoint that's not often heard from pro-life or pro-choice camps."

—Sharon A. Learn, M.A., Age 70
Chief Operations Officer (Retired)
West Chester, PA

"A must read for any female, regardless of age. Dr. Bellanger addresses questions that I'd passed off as insignificant or incidental, answering them in the most honest, easy-to-understand way. The 'Loose Lips' chapter is required reading for us mature women! This book is also a must read for any young woman who is nervous or needing insight regarding her first visit to a gynecologist. I'm buying copies for all my young nieces and my daughter."

—Bernadette Fricchione, Age 58
Teacher
New York, NY

"*Confessions of a Male Gynecologist* is enlightening, from Dr. Bellanger's account of the training it takes to become a doctor and his look at medicine as a business, to his insight into the Affordable Care Act and abuse of the health care system. This book also demonstrates why it really is necessary to discuss everything with your doctor— there's probably nothing they haven't already heard. "

—Judy Wheeler, Age 67
Career Advisor (Semi-retired)
Lowell, MA

"An entertaining look at the issues we physicians face daily, *Confessions of a Male Gynecologist* puts the life and challenges of being a doctor on the table. I very much enjoyed reading and relating to it."

—Dr. Gary Merlino, Age 53
Internal Medicine Physician
Miami Beach, FL

"It's good to know your doctor's perspective, and *Confessions of a Male Gynecologist* reveals what your physician is thinking in a way that's incredibly informative and entertaining. It answers many questions I wouldn't ask my own OBGYN."

—Esperanza Mayer, Age 38
Mother and Wife
Palm Beach, FL

"*Confessions of a Male Gynecologist* is highly readable, informative, and funny. Dr. Bellanger shares stories and insights from his many years as a gynecologist, combining practical medical information with just the right amount of humor. Any woman who sees a gynecologist owes it to herself to read this book."

—Dr. Adam Goodfarb, Age 51
Pediatrician
Los Angeles, CA

"A truly insightful look into the complexity and realities of not only women's health, but the state of our health care system today. An easy read that will change your perspective on what to worry about when going to the gynecologist. Enjoyable and informative, a must read for women of all ages."

—Sarah R. Wolf, Age 37
Registered Nurse
West Palm Beach, FL

To my devoted wife:
You have fostered my aspirations and been by my side
for over thirty years, long before this medical journey began.

The patient was thirty-something weeks pregnant and experiencing some cramping. I wanted to ensure she wasn't having preterm labor, so I performed an internal exam. I felt something in her vagina—something other than normal body parts, that is. It was hard, like metal.

"I need to take a look," I said to the patient, grabbing my speculum. I peered in and saw something shimmering.

I reached in and carefully extracted the shiny item.

"Look what I just found," I said, as the gold chain I'd just pulled out of my patient's vagina dangled from a pair of forceps. I struggled to maintain my composure.

The patient didn't flinch, but stared straight into my eyes. "Oh ... I've been looking for that," she said.

ABOUT THE AUTHOR

Dr. Andre Bellanger has been sitting on the other side of the stirrups for more than two decades. A board-certified obstetrician and gynecologist (OBGYN), he's delivered nearly five thousand babies and cared for tens of thousands of women from all walks of life. He provides a warm and knowledgeable approach to women's health, and for the past five years, he's received the Vitals Patients' Choice Award, an honor that recognizes doctors with the highest scores in bedside manner.

In addition to seeing patients in his private practice, Dr. Bellanger teaches medical students and residents as a clinical adjunct professor. He also serves on the Board of Directors of a large, multi-specialty physicians group, and is Chairman of the Department of Obstetrics and Gynecology at a local hospital. Dr. Bellanger is an avid golfer and enjoys reading, biking, skiing, and traveling. He lives in Florida with his wife and two sons.

CONTENTS

WELCOME TO MY WORLD

Like many people, I've dreamed for years of writing a book—not just any book, mind you, but one that would offer women an uncensored peek behind the curtain (so to speak) of my profession, as well as a glimpse into my perspective not only as a gynecologist, but as a male gynecologist. And truth be told, I had a bit to get off my chest. In 2015, I resolved to turn my dream into reality and started writing—a process that was sometimes more difficult and time-consuming than I'd anticipated. But I had a lot to say, and I wanted to leave it all on the table.

Initially, I planned to call my book *What Your Gynecologist is Really Thinking*, but when I mentioned my working title to several women, they quickly set me straight: They don't necessarily *want* to know what their gynecologist thinks. Rather, they want to know if what they experience is normal—if *they* are normal. While women have become a lot more open about their bodies and sexual health in recent decades, there are still many topics that the majority of these females don't broach with their closest friends, much less with their doctors. But that doesn't mean they aren't curious, or that they don't have important questions that could impact their well-being. So I've tried to shed some light on many of the subjects I've found women wonder about—from surprise pregnancies to piercings to pubic hair.

It's my hope that this book will surprise, entertain, educate, and provoke you. I haven't sugar-coated my writing, and you may be shocked by my blunt observations, but I felt it was important to address each subject with brutal honesty. Each chapter can stand alone, and I encourage you to explore the topics in any order you like. Read the book from beginning to end or turn to the table of contents and seek out the sections that interest you.

At the very least, I hope every female will take away one very important message I've tried to convey: Choose your gynecologist carefully and don't be afraid to speak frankly with him or her at all times. In doing so, I believe you'll find you have absolutely nothing to lose and everything to gain.

So pour your coffee—or your water or your wine—make yourself comfortable, and turn the page. I'm about to offer you an insight into my profession—and your health: a view from the other side of the stirrups.

PAGING DR. GOOGLE

I've realized that when many of my patients schedule an appointment, they're seeking a second opinion—not because they've already seen one of my colleagues, but because they've consulted Dr. Google. Pregnant women, especially those who are expecting for the first time, tend to Google everything. They're directed to blogs, Facebook pages, Wikipedia, and hundreds of other sites. At least once a week a patient presents me with a birth plan she's printed from the Internet. (A birth plan is simply a document describing the patient's wishes when it comes to giving birth. It typically includes a myriad of topics such as whether or not the patient wants meds for pain, what to do with the umbilical cord, if she wants her labor and delivery photographed, etc.) I've had several amusing conversations with patients about these Internet birth plans. It's not uncommon for these exchanges to go something like this:

Patient: "I found this birth plan that suggests giving birth underwater and I'm really excited about it."

Me: "Have you read it?"

Patient: "Well, not all of it."

Me: "Okay, let's look through this together. Do you understand why this birth plan suggests you give birth underwater?"

Patient: "Hmmm. Not really. I Googled 'birth plans' and this one kind of stood out, so I thought maybe I would go with it."

Ah, the wonders of technology, I think to myself.

Me: "Okay, let's talk about the things that are important when it comes to your birth plan. You want to be offered an epidural? Fabulous. You want me to delay cutting the cord? Great, no problem. You want to give birth underwater? Go find a midwife."

Another hot topic—or at least one that many of my patients have brought up—is what they want to actually be doing while they're in labor. "I don't want to be in bed. I want to be walking around when I'm in labor," is something I've heard over and over again.

My reply: "To be honest with you, I don't want you at the hospital when you're in labor and still able to walk around. I want you at the hospital when you're advanced, dilated, and ready to have the baby." I explain that the women they've read about on the Internet, who've claimed they walked around "in labor," were not, in fact, in labor at all. They might have been dilated one centimeter and contracting, but they weren't in labor. Believe me, a woman who's five centimeters and truly in active labor isn't going to be walking around. I'd rather my patients stay at home during early contractions, and come to the hospital only when they're experiencing actual labor. Just ask any woman who's gone through the birthing process: I'm sure she'll tell you that walking around was the last thing she was thinking about when she reached that point.

The Internet is a wonderful innovation, but countless sites contain false and misleading "facts" and recommendations that (unfortunately) some people accept as truth, and Dr. Google serves up unending fantastical and misleading stories for throngs of curious researchers.

When users have so much misinformation available at the stroke of a key, physicians' jobs can be extremely challenging—even more so when the patient is pregnant. "Don't Google, go to our website," I tell my patients over and over again. "That's where you'll find good information." Yet every single day patients who can't resist surfing the web present me with tidbits they've gleaned online. That's not surprising: It's been estimated that eighty-six percent of women self-diagnose via the Internet, and over half self-treat based on online research.[1]

Of course, when it comes to pregnancy, women seem to find all the worst possible scenarios not only on the Internet, but also in books. One book in particular, which shall remain nameless here, scares the bejesus out of every single pregnant patient who reads it. If you experience pressure or a sharp pain, it doesn't mean you're going into preterm labor, have an ectopic pregnancy, or that the baby is in jeopardy. Most of the time, some pressure and pain are normal, but *please* … reach out to your own doctor, *not* Dr. Google.

Making a Mountain Out of a Molehill

Some women also search the Internet whenever they experience an irregularity, pregnant or not. Suddenly, every little ache or spot of blood mushrooms into some form of cancer—ovarian, cervical, or uterine—or another sinister disease. I understand the desire to Google symptoms to get an instant diagnosis, but there's so much misinformation online, people can end up becoming basket cases over nothing. That's why I recommend talking to a physician. A doctor worth his or her salt will listen to your concerns, perform tests if necessary, and determine if further treatment is warranted. Don't you think you'd stand a better chance of getting an accurate diagnosis if you're seen by a real, live physician rather than conducting a Google search that directs you to *randomachesandpains.com*? Dr. Google is not board-certified, does not know your situation, hasn't seen you, and hasn't evaluated you.

Every week, I have patients who know exactly what's wrong, courtesy of a couple of clicks of a mouse. That spot of blood? If it's not cancer, it must be a miscarriage—even if it's merely a red pin prick on a piece of toilet paper that can only be seen with a magnifying glass. The truth is,

---

[1] Holmes Report. (2016). *Women Increasingly Take Charge Of Own Health, Survey Finds.* Retrieved from http://www.holmesreport.com/research/article/women-increasingly-take-charge-of-own-health-survey-finds

miscarrying is fairly common, occurring in roughly one-third of all pregnancies, but women leap to the conclusion unnecessarily, thanks to the Internet. (By the way, if one-third seems high to you, that's because many statistics on miscarriages only count cases in which women know they've lost a pregnancy. Many women miscarry without even realizing they're expecting: Their period may be late and then they have a heavy menses, which, in reality, is a miscarriage.) Spotting can be scary, but miscarriages are usually accompanied by heavy bleeding—and even heavy bleeding doesn't always mean a woman has miscarried. And what if a patient who isn't pregnant is experiencing pelvic discomfort and bloating? Even though it's not all that common, she must have ovarian cancer. It's certainly not because she's constipated or has eaten some fiber-rich food, says Dr. Google.

Furthermore, many patients think they know precisely which treatment they need thanks to the sage counsel of all-knowing Dr. Google. A patient's boyfriend is experiencing burning and now she has itching. According to certain websites, disaster's certainly lurking in the shadows. She tells me, "I know I have chlamydia ... I want the pill and not the cream." Another woman has self-diagnosed an infection: She informs me exactly what type of infection it is, and how it should be treated. Yet another patient is early into her pregnancy and has a sharp pain. No doubt about it, she's having an ectopic pregnancy—a pregnancy in the fallopian tubes—and needs to rush to the hospital. Forget the fact that pregnancy stretches the uterus, which is basically a large muscle, and all that stretching can cause cramps. So when she arrives in my office she declares—before I even begin to examine her—that she wants the injectable treatment for her ectopic pregnancy rather than surgery. Never mind that she hasn't been diagnosed and there's a good chance she doesn't need treatment at all. And still another patient is certain she has PID (Pelvic Inflammatory Disease). She advises me she will have to be put on a course of antibiotics and there's a chance she will have to be hospitalized. Hmm, I think to myself. *This woman has been married for twenty years and is in a monogamous relationship. PID is seen only in women who have a sexually transmitted disease and multiple sexual partners. She must have consulted Dr. Google before coming to see me.*

An Expert on Every Page

Pregnant women often are immunocompromised. This means their immune systems are weakened and they're not as capable of fighting off illness as they are when they're not pregnant. So two people—mother and child—are at risk when a pregnant patient catches an infection. A few years ago, two pregnant women in my community became sick with the flu and died. I once had to perform an emergency C-section on an ill patient at thirty-two weeks. She ended up intubated on a breathing device in intensive care—another victim of the flu. These tragic events—and others like them—should *never* happen, but each day social media users continually post negative comments discouraging people from getting flu shots and describing in detail all the terrible reactions that could occur. Unfortunately, some readers buy into these untruths and refuse to inoculate against the virus—with potentially deadly consequences.

Social media has created a lot of "experts." If you spend any amount of time on Facebook, you probably know exactly what I mean: Scores of people freely spout off about everything, and when they're not posting their own opinions, they're often reposting articles they received from unreliable sources. Compounding this is the fact that many social media users join groups based on their ideals, like pro- and anti-vaccination pages. This means the information they read is biased to reinforce the opinions they've already formed, rather than based on facts.

Yet regardless of which side of the coin you're on, the best source of information is your personal physician. I'm always glad when patients ask my opinion about immunizations like a flu shot, though I never try to force them. I merely tell them the truth—the facts based on reputable research and extensive experimentation conducted by highly qualified scientists and physicians. And I don't sugarcoat my words. "Here's why you need this shot," I say. "Here are the pros. There aren't really any downsides. I know you're worried about this, but the flu shot is not going to cause your child to have autism, and it's not going to give you the flu. Those are myths. The flu vaccine isn't a live vaccine. I don't want to see you get sick; I don't want you to end up in intensive care; I don't want you to die. But if you decide not to do it, that's okay because this is America and you get to choose."

While we're at it, I have another pet peeve that relates to a different form of media: television. I don't believe pharmaceutical companies should be allowed to advertise medications on TV. I'm thoroughly against it. Ad agencies are skilled at creating demand for a brand by portraying happy, healthy, beautiful people whose lives have been improved by the product they're pushing—from protein shakes to miracle cures—for maladies ranging from psoriasis to erectile dysfunction and everything in between.

These ads manipulate emotions, and people often don't take the time to analyze the research data. For instance, the FDA has just approved a new medication that's supposed to increase a woman's sexual desire. According to the study, the medicine was effective in just four percent of women involved in the study, and their desire only increased by ten percent. Those figures are pretty minimal, yet I guarantee when the ads appear on TV, this drug will be in high demand, regardless of its potentially significant side effects.

So perhaps we as a society need to step back and reconsider the health decisions we make based on what we learn from mass media. Curiosity's not a bad thing; neither are the Internet, television, books, or magazines. People just need to use common sense when they click on a site, read a book, or see something on television that offers information or advice. My request to all women, not just my patients, is if you're going to use various types of media as a resource, read and digest the material before presenting it to your OBGYN. No recommendation is a one-size-fits-all solution. Decide what makes sense to you, and then discuss it with your doctor.

TO SHAVE OR NOT TO SHAVE? THAT IS THE QUESTION

If I had a nickel for every time a patient said to me, "I'm sorry, I didn't shave my legs," I'd be a very wealthy man.

My standard response is to make a joke out of it and say, "That's okay, I won't look. I promise I won't tell anyone." But the reality is it doesn't matter to me or any other OBGYN because it's not your legs we're examining. Hairy legs have no impact on how we perform the exam. So there's no need to worry, and you certainly don't need to apologize.

From my perspective, there's very little pubic hair left in the state of Florida. Fifteen years ago, no one shaved their private parts. But that's changed. About ten years ago, I noticed that many of my patients began "trimming" their pubic area. At first, I was a bit puzzled, but when I thought about it, the whole thing kind of made sense. People have experimented with new looks on every other part of their bodies for years—tattoos, hairstyles, beards, nail designs, colored contact lens, pierced ears—so why not a new look for the pubic area? And what started out as trimming seems to have evolved into a "bald is beautiful" movement. Today in my practice, I'd estimate that ninety-eight percent of my patients under the age of fifty shave or wax their private parts completely. (To be honest, I have no idea if these women are shaving or waxing and I don't care—I'm happy for that aspect of female grooming to remain a mystery to me.) Of those over fifty, I'd say about sixty percent totally remove their pubic hair; but in general, the older my patients are, the less they adhere to this practice. It's not a topic I discuss with my patients, but I find the shaving/waxing trend fascinating. Of course, my statistics reflect only the patients in my practice, and I do live in Florida where women wear bathing suits almost year round—so perhaps that's why so many women choose to go bare down there. Maybe women in cold climates, like Minnesota, don't shave. I don't know.

I have to admit, it's much easier to do a gynecologic exam when there's no hair in the way, so I'd encourage any of you who are considering shaving or waxing to go right ahead and do it. I don't want to sound crude, but when I have to fight my way through a jungle to check what I need to check, the exam sometimes takes longer—and I don't think I've ever had a patient who's wanted to spend a minute more in those stirrups than she's had to. So if you're wondering, "Hmm ... Should I shave down there?" my answer is, "Go for it!" If you want to shave your legs while you're at it, that's entirely up to you—but as I said earlier, you didn't make a gynecologic appointment to have your legs examined, and we're not giving out prizes for smoothest legs.

THE AIR DOWN THERE

Frankly, I don't know of an OBGYN who thinks twice about treating patients who don't shave their legs or private parts, and it might surprise you to know we also don't care if you haven't had a chance to shower before an appointment. You're not in high school gym anymore, where the coach stands in the locker room and makes sure you shower before your next class, so relax. We don't have a checklist of "does she or doesn't she" boxes we tick before we examine you. We're only in that area for a minute or two, and we're not looking to see whether you showered or not. It's no big deal. I've had a lot of patients who've showered and scrubbed every inch of their bodies before their appointment, and when they get to my office, they're asked to provide a urine sample before I see them. Off they go into the restroom, where they do as they're asked. What they don't realize is they've left behind what we call in the trade "toilet paper tornadoes"—lots of them—and that's the first thing I see when I begin my exam. But that's okay. My staff and I have seen just about everything, and we really don't sit around and obsess about how gross the sight is because, to us, it's not. Whether or not you're clean as a whistle or have little flecks of toilet paper decorating your genitals, the state of your private parts doesn't upset us or change how we feel about you as a person. We don't think, "Oh my goodness! She's a toilet paper magnet! She's dirty, and she doesn't know how to clean herself." We get it. We understand. We're not judging you.

That's not to say we can't smell the different odors coming from our patients' bodies, both good and bad. We do. For example, take the woman who works and can only come in for an appointment at the end of the day. She doesn't have time for a shower, and that's okay. We're not going to turn her away. In Florida, lots of women wear shoes without socks, and guess what? Their feet smell! But I'm not going to walk into the exam room with a clothespin on my nose or fan the air with my hand. Nor am I going to make fun of a patient after she leaves and exclaim, "Whew! That stink was killing me!" Smells are just part of the world we OBGYNs live in, and we know better than to base our opinion of a patient's hygiene or likeability on her smell. It's funny if you think about it: there'd be a lot fewer podiatrists, dentists, proctologists, and gastroenterologists if everyone chose their area of specialty based on smell alone. That's why I'm amused when a woman rushes in without showering and worries about being stinky. I'm more than happy she's made her appointment on time and didn't cancel because she didn't have time to shower. Better to deal with a smelly patient than none at all.

Since I'm being completely truthful, though, there are times when I'll smell a patient's foot odor or see toilet paper tornadoes and wish she'd had time to clean up a bit before coming in. I'll look at my nurse, who's in the room assisting me, and she'll look at me. Each of us knows the other is chuckling inside because we're thinking the same thing. And some of those things just strike me as funny. I love my patients and I love a good laugh. I'd never want to embarrass any of them with inappropriate reactions. But I'm also only human, and when I see, hear, or smell some things, they amuse me. Like I said earlier, it doesn't matter if a patient shaves her legs before her appointment; but when a patient comes in and hoists up legs that are hairier than any man's, I'm going to notice and I wonder what her significant other thinks about her membership in the shaggy limbs club. I'll chuckle to myself and I may even smile about it for the rest of the day. But I'm not going to think less of her for it, and it certainly doesn't affect my job.

We have patients who represent all points in the spectrum. Some are ultra-meticulous about their appearance and hygiene. You know the type: They shower and powder before they'll even answer the doorbell. These women would rather be caught dead than be seen with perspiration stains under their arms. Then there are their counterparts from the opposite end of the scale. Either they can't be bothered with personal hygiene issues or they're allergic to soap and water. Who knows? Most patients fall somewhere in between, but all are welcome, even the cleanliness-challenged ones.

I've seen all types, of course, and have observed just about everything a doctor could possibly witness during exams. This may seem gross—in fact, readers with weak constitutions might want to skip the remainder of this paragraph—but I've conducted lots of examinations where women accidentally pooped while I was down in that region, or they'd hadn't cleaned themselves well after a bowel movement earlier in the day. Some of those patients are the very women who appear perfectly groomed at all times—at least on the outside— and I'm sure they'd be horrified to know I've seen parts of them that were less than pristine. It only goes to show that what you see isn't always what you get.

BECOMING AN OBGYN

I was ten years old when I decided I wanted to be a doctor. For as long as I can remember, my dad encouraged me: "You should become a doctor," he always used to say. I wasn't following an established family tradition; in fact, there were no "professionals" in my immediate family up to that point. So I'm sure my parents took a lot of pleasure in the idea of their son becoming the first to achieve this distinction. After all, what parent doesn't take great pride in referring to their child as "my son (or daughter), the doctor?" Dad worked in retail, in a position that involved multiple transfers, so my family moved a lot. I remember thinking if I became a physician, I wouldn't have to move all the time. Of course, that wasn't my only motivation, but when I was young, the thought of staying in one place was appealing. My parents planted the seed, and I nurtured the idea until it blossomed into a concrete goal—and that goal became a reality.

I didn't achieve my objective overnight, though. After four years of college, I took a two-year detour, attended grad school, and earned a master's degree in health administration (MHA). My next choices launched my personal and professional life in new directions. First, I married my high school sweetheart. We'd gone to our high school prom together and had attended the same college in the Northeast. Now that I had my MHA, we were ready to tie the knot. Around the same time, I was accepted to a medical school in Florida. So after we wed, we packed up and moved to the Sunshine State, and looked forward to a fresh, exciting start as newlyweds. We knew med school would be a challenge, but we were young and in love and could handle everything life threw at us.

And we did, but life wasn't all rainbows and roses. The first two years of medical school are brutally difficult and intensive for students and their families. Most schools, like the one I attended, allow very little time for personal life outside of learning. Just ask my wife—she'll be the first person to tell you that when I was in medical school and residency, she considered herself a widow because she almost never saw me. I was on a regimented schedule without any leeway during those years: Class attendance was mandatory, and my classes met for seven or eight hours a day, five days a week; however, I wasn't free to go home and relax at the end of each day of classes. Instead, I'd get home around 5:00 p.m., share a quick dinner, and head to the library to study for three or four hours every single night. By the time the weekend arrived, I was exhausted, but still with no end in sight: Saturdays just meant extra hours to cram in additional study time, usually eight or more hours.

The pace is cruel, but these first two years of extreme pressure are necessary. Doctors, regardless of their specialty, must retain mountains of information about the human body, and medical students have a lot to learn. That's one of the reasons medical schools are so selective. Not to toot my own horn, but getting into med school isn't easy. They accept the candidates they consider to be most qualified, which means med schools can pick and choose among the best and the brightest. Applicants who make the cut don't just sit back and rely on their past achievements. It's an extremely competitive environment, and they study hard and push themselves to excel.

Students make the transition from classroom to clinical rotation during their third year of medical school—and that's when they really learn to be physicians. The third and fourth years are still very challenging, but a little more fun. Students spend a month or six weeks in a core sub-specialty (such as internal medicine, surgery, family practice, emergency medicine, and obstetrics and gynecology among others); usually, during rotation, they get a feel for the area in which they want to specialize. I recall doing a rotation in OBGYN and thinking, *I never want to do this. I see these fifty-something-year-old doctors dragging themselves into the hospital at three o'clock in the morn-*

ing, and they look like death warmed over. I don't want to be there. So what specialty did I choose? You guessed it. Fortunately, I also witnessed the other side: the extraordinary relationships these docs established with their patients. OBGYN docs see their patients year after year after year. While going to the gynecologist can sometimes be a daunting or fearful event, many women develop enduring, trusting rapport with these physicians.

Three factors influenced me to ultimately specialize in OBGYN: the special doctor-patient relationships I observed, the satisfaction I received from performing surgery and delivering babies, and becoming a father myself. During my second year of medical school, my wife got pregnant and underwent a significant complication during pregnancy. Her issue both concerned and fascinated me, and I admired the way her doctor handled it. Everything worked out great, and we had a beautiful son. Another beautiful son followed a few years later.

My first son was born during my third year in medical school. After my fourth year, I did what all future doctors do: apply for residency. Essentially, it's applying for a job, though the process is very different from applying for a traditional job where applicants are hired or not hired. In the United States, the National Resident Matching Program, or NRMP, is used to match applicants and medical institutions. Candidates who successfully complete med school apply and interview at anywhere between five and ten teaching hospitals throughout the U.S., and then rank those hospitals in their order of preference. At the same time, the hospitals rank their applicants, and the NRMP performs a match. Applicants are obligated to join the residency program at whatever hospital is a match—which is crazy in some ways. It's kind of like the NFL draft: all these football players make it through college, and they're eager to play pro football, but they could end up playing for a team anywhere in the United States.

If you're a fan of evening hospital soap operas, you may have developed preconceived notions about the lives of residents or what it's like to work in a hospital. I call these programs soap operas because they don't depict the truth very well, if at all: Residency isn't "fun" the way it's portrayed on those shows. You do make good friends because, let's face it, you spend fourteen hours a day with the same people—but it's not fun. Nor will you see patients in labor in the ER, or a first-year surgeon doing cardiac surgery. I must say, however, that the two evening hospital shows I've watched occasionally are on target from a medical perspective regarding the issues and the solutions. And by the way, residents do get paid, but very little. I remember figuring out my hourly wage back when I was a resident. I think I earned $4.00 an hour, less than the federal minimum wage at that time.

I ended up in a residency program in a large Northeast metropolitan city, which was a great training experience because inner-city hospitals provide care for many indigent, uninsured patients with a wide variety of problems. Believe me, I saw a lot and learned even more. An OBGYN residency is a four-year program with intense exposure to general obstetrics and gynecology, as well as exposure to subspecialties, such as gynecologic oncology, fetal medicine, and infertility. I can tell you from experience that starting interns get stuck with the lowest form of drudge work and the worst hours. When I was an intern, I normally worked between eighty and a hundred twenty hours each week, and each shift was grueling.

I started work every day at 6:00 a.m. and didn't get home until 6:00 p.m. or later. Every fourth night, when I was on call, I was required to stay at the hospital all night and report for duty the following morning at six. I couldn't sleep until my twelve-hour shift was completed, and by then, it was all I could do to stagger home and collapse into bed. I delivered ten to twelve babies a day, and several each night that I was on call. Those were some tough years, for my wife, for me, and for our sons. I'd come home and, before I knew it, I'd be sound asleep with a baby on my lap. I also had household duties to take care of. I remember times in the Northeast when I mowed the lawn with my younger son toddling behind me pushing his little plastic bubble mower. That was "our" time: We had to work around my schedule—but somehow we managed.

Thankfully, regulations controlling the number of hours an intern can work are now in place, and future doctors are no longer as sleep-deprived as I once was. I won't go so far as to say an intern's workload is easier nowadays, but it's certainly less rigorous. Yet there's no question in my mind that those who complete an OBGYN residency today aren't as well-trained as they were fifteen years ago: They don't see or experience as much, and most aren't prepared to stay up the entire night with emergencies and then see patients all the next day— but they need to be. There aren't a whole lot of jobs tailored to a resident's ideal schedule: mainly, fewer nights on call and having the ability to take the day off after being on call. They should be prepared for reality. The everyday world of an OBGYN often involves working throughout the night and seeing thirty scheduled patients the following day. (Many physicians see as many as fifty patients a day. Frankly, there is no way any OBGYN who's seeing that many patients can give each one the attention she needs. More on this in the chapter on wellness exams.)

Residents start the four-year program learning to perform simple tasks and progress to more complex assignments as they master each skill. They shoulder more responsibilities, participate in increasingly complicated surgical procedures, and engage in in-office practice. Those with more experience under their belts may even oversee other residents. At the culmination of the program, residents take a written board exam and, once they pass, they can finally step out into the real world as independent doctors. As in many situations, though, there's a catch. Passing a written exam doesn't mean the doctor is board-certified but merely board-eligible. There's still one final hurdle to jump: The new doctor must practice for a specific period of time—for an OBGYN, it's two years—and document all patient cases during that period before taking an oral exam to become a board-certified doctor.

I joined an established doctor's practice in the Northeast after my residency and stayed in that practice for three years. As a new physician, I was required to enter information into a computer program for every single patient I encountered during my first two years. My records were detailed and thorough. For example, if I performed surgery, I had to include the indication (reason) for the surgery, the procedure, the pathology, the outcome, and if there were complications. Of course, that included deliveries: from basic vaginal deliveries to more problematic ones involving the use of forceps or vacuum or C-sections. It didn't matter how simple or complicated the procedure was, everything had to be painstakingly documented. When my two years of board-eligible time were up, I sat for my oral boards. I'd spent an enormous chunk of my life trying to achieve my dream, and I was now in the final stretch: All I needed to do was hold it together for one last sprint. Did I say sprint? Orals were more like a marathon. A panel of doctors reviewed everything I'd documented during the past twenty-four months and questioned me about random cases for four arduous hours. The process was exhausting and nerve-wracking, and I thought it would never end. At some point, though, they must have decided my documentation and answers were acceptable because I passed. I was a board-certified physician.

I practiced in the Northeast for another year while my wife and I discussed making one more move. A bit older and wiser, we decided to return to Florida, this time to set down roots. I established my own practice sixteen years ago and have worked there since.

SEX ED HOTLINE

My son decided to pledge a fraternity during his first year of college, and he proudly told the fraternity brothers I was an OB-GYN. Naturally, most of the guys reacted to this news the way many young males do: "Oh, a gynecologist? Cool! Like, your dad gets to look at naked women all day." Of course, the brothers couldn't pass up the chance to gather some pearls of wisdom from a qualified source and put a few questions of their own to rest. It would usually happen on a Friday night around nine o'clock after they'd had a few drinks. One of the guys would tell my son, "We need to ask your dad questions. How about getting him on the phone?"

My son, being a pledge, was compelled to do their bidding. He was a bit nervous about disturbing me the first time, but I took it all in stride. My phone would ring, and I'd hear my son ask, "Dad, have you got a few minutes? A few of the guys have some questions." What followed was a barrage of inquiries about sex, STDs, condoms, the best ways to protect themselves and their partners from unwanted pregnancies, and so on. I didn't mind at all. I found it kind of funny that they'd let a parent into their inner circle—at least by phone—when they had a bit of a buzz, and I was glad they weren't afraid to bring up topics most adults would rather run from than discuss.

Of course, I think some of their questions were designed to shock me. I envisioned six or eight fraternity brothers sitting around on the floor, drinking beer, and trying to come up with questions, each one edgier than the last. Although I couldn't see them, I imagined my son's friends trying to grab the phone from one another and saying, "My turn. Lemme ask him this." To them it was just a big joke and the guys were trying to push it to the extreme.

They had so many truly funny ways of asking things, and I wish I'd written them all down. Some of their most memorable questions have stood out in my mind simply because they were so crude and hysterical.

The guys were interested in what I did each day and would ask me to explain. Usually, the next question went like this:

Frat Brother: "Well, you know, you're seeing pussy all day and doesn't that get you excited?"

Me: "No, it's a job. It's what I do for a living. It doesn't get me excited." And I'd be thinking: *I doubt they'd understand if I told them I get excited at the prospect of getting eight solid hours of uninterrupted sleep.*

Some college kids hear myths, and unless they find out otherwise, they believe some pretty weird things. One of my son's frat brothers had obviously never been with an Asian woman, but he'd heard they have a rather unique anatomy. I swear he asked me this:

Frat Brother: "Does an Asian woman's vagina go sideways?"

Me: "Nope, they're just like other women." And I'd think: *I hope he's not majoring in Asian studies.*

They'd also ask me things I thought everyone over the age of thirteen knew.

Frat Brother: "Well, if I just get a blow job, can the girl get pregnant?"

Me: "No, that's not how you become a father." And I'd think: *Really? You're really asking me that?*

No matter how my week had gone, whenever my son called and asked if his friends could ask more questions, I knew I'd be laughing after the conversation.

My son's girlfriend was a member of a sorority, and when he told her about these Friday night phone calls, I got another call from him asking if his girlfriend and her sorority sisters could call and ask some questions. The girls weren't drunk and had much more relevant, thoughtful questions than the guys. Like the brothers, they were concerned about pregnancy and STDs, but their questions were smarter, and I could tell they were seriously looking for answers. I imagined them sitting around a table with a written list of questions, politely taking turns speaking.

I think the girls really saw our phone conversations as opportunities to get answers from an expert who didn't know them—someone they didn't have to sit across from and look directly in the eyes. They were more or less anonymous and liked keeping it that way. They asked commonsensical questions—some the same questions as the boys—but phrased in a more (ahem) delicate manner. They also asked when they should start seeing a gynecologist, and had questions about birth control pills, ovarian cysts, and missed or heavy periods. And they inquired about the morning-after pill. They asked about a lot of different things, but most of the time, the conversation returned to pregnancy.

I can't diagnose people over the phone, but I had several conversations that went like this, with the same reply—"See your gynecologist."

Sorority Sister: "I've missed periods. What does that mean?"

Me: "You know, sometimes a missed period can be okay, but if that persists, you need to call your gynecologist."

Sorority Sister: "My periods are heavy ... I have a lot of cramping ... what should I do?"

Me: "You need to call your gynecologist."

The fraternity boys and sorority girls used different tones when asking questions, but I never felt bothered when either group called. The guys made me laugh, and the girls made me feel as if they were seeking answers to pertinent questions. I was happy to enlighten them. Surprisingly, both asked me one question I never saw coming:

"You can't get pregnant if you have anal sex, right?"

Me: "No, no, and no!"

Although I never put them on speakerphone, I'd tell my wife the highlights of my conversations with the kids, and we'd laugh at some of the questions until our stomachs hurt. My sons are a bit older now, no longer in college, and I sort of miss those conversations. Ah, the naïveté of youth.

A DAY IN THE LIFE

The structure of my workday hasn't changed all that much in my more than two decades of medical practice. I get up every day around 6:00 a.m.—assuming I'm not already up because I delivered a baby or had an emergency call in the early morning hours. I enjoy a cup of coffee while reading *The Wall Street Journal* and then head to the office, arriving around 7:30 a.m. My first patient is scheduled for 8:30 a.m., so I have some quiet time to review the charts of the day's patients. This isn't something all docs do, but it's important to me to have a sense of the patients I'll see during the day: I look at their history and my notes from their previous visit to determine if there's anything out of the ordinary I need to address when I see them. The hour I take to review patient charts helps me establish an individual connection with each woman who comes into my office. I know who each patient is and any issues they face before I even walk in the door of the exam room, and I want them to know I care about their concerns. I'm prepared, and I believe being prepared makes me a better doctor.

I see patients from 8:30 a.m. until noon, and then again from 1:00 p.m. until 5:00 p.m. My partner and I have intentionally created a bit of a boutique practice: There's no double or triple booking in our office; our goal isn't to see as many patients we possibly can each day. Rather, we're focused on the quality of care we provide. Typically, we limit the number of patients we see on a given day to twenty—or twenty-five at most on a busy day—as opposed to the thirty-five or forty patients per day scheduled by most practices. For us, it's not about the numbers, but the individual. A patient deserves time with her doctor; but more importantly, we can provide the best care only if we have an adequate amount of time with each patient.

Although scheduled office visits consume a large portion of my day, I have to address many unplanned matters that crop up during and after office hours. My partner and I have patients in the hospital we must attend to; it's not uncommon to receive a call from the nurse caring for one of our patients who's in labor. Typically, the nurse is calling with a question that requires an immediate response—in which case, our office nurses must interrupt us. Like it or not, when babies decide to make their first appearance in the world, they usually don't accommodate the doctors' (or parents') schedules. There's nothing my partner and I can do about it except head to the hospital for the delivery. Sometimes, this means we have to leave during regular office hours when we have patients waiting to see us. We don't like inconveniencing our scheduled patients, so we've hired a qualified nurse practitioner in order to give our patients a choice: They can reschedule or keep their appointments, seeing the nurse practitioner instead of the doctor. Our staff also calls the patients who are on the schedule for the next couple of hours to let them know their appointments will need to be changed. Bottom line: We try to bend over backward to accommodate our patients.

At the end of the day, a physician's practice is a business, and like any business, things happen: the computer server goes down, the printer breaks, a staff member calls in sick. In the course of a day, plenty of other business-related concerns arise that play out behind the scenes, but I can't let these problems affect the quality of care my patients deserve. I may have calls to return and an office manager who has a list of items that need my attention, but my foremost responsibility is to my patients. All other issues can be addressed between patients or whenever I have a few minutes of free time.

That "free time" is usually my lunch hour—from noon to 1:00 p.m., and it's not often I actually get to use those minutes to eat. If I'm running late with patients, I work through lunch. Sometimes, I spend the hour making rounds at the hospital. If my patient delivered the day before, I must see her the following day to ensure she's doing well and update her chart. I prefer to do my rounds early in the morning before office hours, but it's not always possible—and that leaves my lunchtime or evening. When I'm unable to get to the hospital early in the morning and my lunch schedule is full, I make rounds at 5:30 p.m. There are times when one of my patients is admitted to the hospital by her primary care physician for a specific illness, and her doctor discovers an additional problem related to my specialty. In that case, I'll make sure to include her during rounds.

Between rounds, case reviews, office visits, deliveries, emergencies, on-call duty, and overseeing the business aspects of my practice, I put in some very long—but rewarding—days. Of course, as is the case in any profession, some days are a walk in the park and others seem to go on endlessly. But when I think about the babies I've delivered and the joy on the face of each patient as she holds her child for the first time, those long hours seem worth it.

Being on Call

My partner and I take turns being on call for a full week at a time. Whoever's on call takes after-hours phone queries from patients and handles deliveries and emergencies. I've received calls covering a wide range of concerns: one patient has a headache; another thinks she's in labor; someone's water breaks; still others have urinary tract infections or herpes outbreaks for which I need to prescribe medication. On a typical evening when I'm on call, I receive two or three phone calls, and it's really not a big deal. I want to speak with the patient who thinks she's in labor. I also want to help other women whose problems can't wait. But calls at three o'clock in the morning from a patient who tells me she's having trouble sleeping sort of get to me. After all, I'm human, and at that time of the morning, it's tough for me to muster up much of a sense of humor about the irony of the patient's complaint. (More on this in the next chapter.)

When you're on call, you're on call; it's just a fact of life for an OB-GYN, and it pretty much never ends. The doctor on call is responsible whether it's answering questions from patients by phone or going to the hospital when a patient is in labor and performing the delivery—no matter how long it takes or the time of night. Our practice does about twenty deliveries per month, which is certainly manageable for us. With that amount of deliveries, there's almost always a patient or two in the hospital, though numbers can vary on any given day. We've had as few as one patient and as many as six in the hospital at a time. Of course, some on-call weeks are killers: I might be up all night two nights in a row—that's not uncommon, especially since our office is on call for the emergency room (ER) of our local hospital several times a month. My partner and I each put up with a tough week of being on call, and then we enjoy a "normal" week. And now that we have our nurse practitioner on board with us, she takes calls two nights a week to deal with the simpler issues. But if the ER calls, or if a patient is in labor, either my partner or I must respond.

When I'm on call, I never know when I'll get a text message. (For those readers who have been around since the days of pagers, type-writers, and rotary telephones, you may know that pagers have become obsolete. Nowadays, docs get text messages on their cell phones.) I live in Florida and enjoy boating, but I certainly can't go out on a boat during the weeks I'm on call. Nor can I take any type of day trip. I have to stay local because I could be called in at any time. If my wife and I are going out and I have someone in labor, we always take two cars. Not that I'm complaining. I've chosen this life and this is just our normal.

Deliveries

I'm in my early fifties and think of myself as young, but I have to admit, I've changed over the years. When I was in my late twenties and early thirties, I thought nothing about jumping out of bed in the wee hours of the morning to perform a delivery, then returning home an hour or two later and crawling back into bed to grab a bit more sleep. I was sawing logs again before my head touched the pillow. Today, I have no problem rushing out for a call at seven o'clock at night and falling asleep when I return home; but when I get a call at three o'clock in the morning and hurry to the hospital to do a delivery, returning home and falling back to sleep is almost impossible. I just lie in bed and stare at the ceiling until it's time to get up and start the day. I believe my wakefulness is due, in part, to the years and years I've spent waiting for my pager to go off or a text message to come in. Receiving that call when I'm fast asleep in my comfortable bed, then suffering from insomnia when I return home sometimes takes the edge off my enthusiasm for my profession. Still, I'm quite lucky that I love what I do and enjoy being with my patients.

Family Life

Our two sons are now twenty-two and twenty-five. As the boys were growing up, my wife made sure that family time was a priority—and it still is. We usually had dinner together, unless a patient happened to be in labor during the dinner hour. To this day, if I have to make rounds or see a patient after hours, I try to get home by 6:30 p.m., even if I have to go back for a delivery in a couple of hours. There are interruptions and exceptions at times, but it's all about priorities.

It's the same with finding time to exercise and take care of myself. I don't have to do rounds morning, noon, and night, so I do manage to eke out some "me" time. And during the weeks that I'm not on call, I dance to and from work. Well, not really, but I sort of feel footloose and fancy free after putting in countless hours the week before. When I have only one patient in the hospital, I'll see her as early as 7:00 a.m., get to the office with plenty of time to review charts before I see my first patient, and then have my lunch hour and evening free. So no matter how tiring or stressful a particular week gets, I know there's a better one just around the corner.

DON'T I KNOW YOU?

When my son turned twenty-one, he chose to celebrate (as many red-blooded American males do) by going to a strip club and having a few drinks. I was flattered when he invited me to go with him and his friends—after all, how many sons want their old man along for their twenty-first birthday bash?—and I didn't think twice about going. Mind you, I don't make a habit of visiting strip clubs, but hey, it was my son's special night, and I was glad to be a part of it. We drove to a popular joint about half an hour from my home, made our way into the dimly lit club, and found a place to sit. Several scantily clad young women who seemed determined to strip down to their birthday suits gyrated on lighted platforms above the crowd. We had a few rounds of drinks and were enjoying the evening when one of the practically nude dancers sashayed down the ramp, leaned over, and whispered in my son's ear. My son seemed a bit uncomfortable as he glanced at me for a second, nodded, and said something to her. I figured one of his buddies had let the manager know it was his birthday, and the dancer was just giving him a little bit of special attention. Instead, she straightened up, turned to me, and said, "Hey, Dr. Bellanger." Then, with an exaggerated sway of the hips, she sauntered off.

I was mortified. Completely mortified. I realized I'd delivered this woman's baby, was familiar with her most intimate parts. And there I was in a club watching her strip. I wish I could have explained I was only at the club because of my son's birthday, but that excuse sounded pretty lame and, besides, I didn't get the chance. Great. My son later told me that my patient hadn't been whispering sweet nothings in his ear, but had asked, "Is that Dr. Bellanger you're with?" And being the truthful person his mom and I had raised him to be, he'd replied, "Ah ... yeah." Believe it or not, that's the one time I've ever run into a patient in public and have been embarrassed about it.

I live in a relatively small community, which shrinks and grows as snowbirds travel to and from their summer homes in the north. In winter, the population balloons to as many as seventy thousand people; but in the summer, the numbers dramatically decrease, and I'm more likely to run into patients. I see many in public—at the mall, dining in restaurants, at events, just about everywhere I go—and most of my encounters are pleasant.

Some patients recognize me and seem genuinely happy to see me, but others who bump into me can't quite put their finger on who I am—even though I look familiar to them. I get a real kick out of that when it happens.

The patient will frequently say, "I know you from somewhere, but I can't remember exactly where."

My standard response is always the same. "You really don't want to know," I say.

Of course, they keep pressing me, and I finally tell them exactly where they've met me. I get some pretty funny responses: Their jaw drops, their face turns beet red, and they're so embarrassed they typically have trouble saying anything else—especially if they're with other people. I always grin and tell them how much I've enjoyed seeing them before I continue on my way.

The truth of the matter is there are people who approach me whose faces I recognize, but I can't remember their names. I've had lots of women come through my doors over the years, and I'm not exactly focusing on faces during their office visits, so I just assume the person's a patient, whether she is or not. And if she has a hard time remembering who I am, I launch into my "routine." I can't help it. I'm not trying to be mean, but the response I get keeps me smiling for days.

Something else that makes me chuckle is when a patient approaches me with her husband in tow and says, "Hi, Dr. Bellanger. How are you? It's so nice to see you." She smiles as if I'm her best friend, and I'm glad she feels we have a good relationship. Then she introduces her husband to me, saying, "Honey, this is my gynecologist, Dr. Bellanger." Oftentimes, the husband isn't all that thrilled to meet me. After all, we share a common ground he may not be comfortable sharing. I'm used to receiving glares from my patient's significant other, but sometimes I get the opposite reaction: the husband suddenly takes an interest in the floor or the ceiling, but refuses to look me in the eye as he mumbles an unintelligible response, takes his wife's arm, and firmly leads her away.

Another response I get a lot is from patients who recognize me, but are mortified to bump into me in public. They don't know how to acknowledge me and sometimes go out of their way to avoid me. Suddenly, that taillight displayed in the auto accessories shop window is the most interesting thing on earth, and they turn their backs to me, remaining still as a statue, seemingly transfixed by that small auto part. Naturally, I walk right up to them just to see their reaction when I say, "Hey, imagine seeing you here. How are you?" I can tell they're thinking that if they had a shovel they'd dig themselves a hole and crawl right in. I always wonder if they'd avoid me if I were their Ear, Nose and Throat specialist.

I'm a visual person. I recognize most people, but I admit I'm not very good with names. Years ago, before we had electronic records, my staff took Polaroids of my patients' faces during their first visit so they'd be in the charts when I reviewed them the morning of their visit. It really helped me keep names, faces, and conditions linked. Electronic records make that process even easier today. Instead of Polaroids, we use digital cameras. Still, when I'm out and about, I can't remember everyone; but if my wife's with me, she acts as my wingman. When a patient greets me, and I pause a bit before responding, my wife will step in and say, "Hi, I'm Sherri, and you are … ?" It's a perfectly natural way to get the patient to say her name without embarrassing either of us. Thank goodness my wife's got my back when in these situations.

Many patients come in for their yearly visits and say to me, "I saw you at the mall," or wherever they saw me.

My reply is always the same. "Well, why didn't you come say hello?"

Characteristically, they say, "I didn't want to bother you with your family," or, "I was embarrassed to say hello."

It's funny how some patients are embarrassed by our doctor-patient relationship and the fact I'm their gynecologist. To me, it's just a fact of life, and I find it amusing. But I remember how uncomfortable I was when the dancer at the strip club recognized and acknowledged me—so I do understand how it feels to have the tables turned.

THE BUSINESS OF MEDICINE

What do physicians have in common with accountants, lawyers, plumbers, and hairdressers? They provide a service for which they're paid. In other words, a doctor's office—or "practice" as we call it—is a business. And just like any other business, we have overhead: insurance, taxes, telephone and Internet, legal and accounting fees, office equipment and supplies, rent, utilities, electricity, water, cleaning services, insurance, technology, and other costs. As in many businesses, labor is our largest expense. Physician assistants and nurse practitioners earn $60,000 to $120,000 per year. We have a nurse practitioner in our office as well as two physicians, a nurse, and eight other employees. The cost of labor includes not only salaries, but benefits such as 401Ks and health insurance. We pay over $6,000 a month to provide health insurance to our employees.

But that's not all. In addition to the expenses that all businesses incur, there are numerous costs particular to a medical practice: medical equipment and maintenance (an ultrasound machine costs $40,000 and hysteroscopy[2] equipment for in-office surgery is $15,000); malpractice insurance, medical waste disposal, upfront costs for supplies such as vaccines ($100 each) and intrauterine devices ($750 each) that we must keep on hand. County regulations require a permit for the office and for each practitioner; the state requires a general license for the practice and an additional license because we perform

---

[2] A hysteroscopy is a procedure in which the OBGYN looks inside the uterus to determine the cause of abnormal bleeding.

in-office surgeries. Because of the strict regulations in the world of medicine, we must hire an IT company that specializes in physician offices—to the tune of $7,500 annually, and that doesn't include any software or hardware upgrades. Even the cost of shredding services is higher than it is for other businesses because of HIPPA regulations.

So there are expenses—lots of them. And, of course, we have income—and hopefully, profit.

Many people believe physicians make money hand over fist, but the business of medicine has become increasingly difficult and less profitable each year. The income in a physician's practice comes from only two sources: co-pays and insurance reimbursement. That's it. You've probably heard that reimbursement to doctors from insurance companies is shrinking thanks to the Affordable Care Act. And as you may be well aware, patient co-pays, co-insurance, and deductibles have risen dramatically in the last several years. It's become a daily battle for doctors to earn a profit. Physicians must not only practice good doctoring, but they have to be "business smart" so they don't lose money and fail at the business side of the practice. These challenges have resulted in increasing numbers of physicians leaving private practice to work for hospitals: The notion of becoming a salaried employee and chucking the headaches associated with owning a business certainly is tempting, and it's easy for me to understand why many doctors choose to go this route.

Better for the Patients, Better for the Doctors

Our office has joined a large group of nearly four hundred OBGYN practices here in Florida, and we practice under the umbrella of that group. This means better care for our patients and more income for the practice.

We believe our member physicians practice better medicine because the group drives good behavior: Doctors must be board-certified, adhere to specific quality standards, and achieve certain goals as documented on quarterly scorecards. Numerous aspects of a physician's practice—specifically related to patients—are recorded and submitted. For example, physicians report their C-section rate, and the number of in-office procedures versus those done at the hospital. (In-office procedures are almost always more comfortable and cost-effective for the patient.) Preventive medicine, including wellness visits versus problem visits and rate of vaccinations, is also documented on the scorecard. All of these parameters are compared not only to those of other doctors in the group, but also to national averages.

One of the primary principles, in place since our group was first formed, is that every patient should be given optimum care regardless of which insurance they have. Specifically, a patient should never be treated differently because of their health insurance. No physician should ever think, *This insurance company doesn't pay enough, so I won't do this procedure or that test.* That attitude has no place in practicing medicine. However, as a group, we do possess the power to negotiate our contracts with insurance companies.

A large portion of the general public may not be aware that physicians negotiate their reimbursement rates with insurance companies. Simply put, the payment your OBGYN receives from XYZ insurance for an annual visit may be different than what a doctor in my practice receives for that same procedure by that same insurance company. The average solo practitioner possesses very little power and is reimbursed at a rate that's similar to the Medicare rate, which is quite low. However, when an insurance company is providing a contract to a group of four hundred physicians, the group is able to negotiate higher reimbursement rates. This is no different than in the non-medical world: There is power in numbers. The large insurance companies must negotiate with us, or risk losing us as a customer; if any insurance company were to lose us as a customer, they wouldn't have enough OBGYNs in Florida. As in any negotiation, there's give and take, though. For example, we ask for higher reimbursement rates in exchange for promising that we'll use in-network labs and hospitals, which saves money for the insurance company. Most hospitals are part of large systems, and they, too, have negotiating power.

Let's say I perform a hysteroscopy at a particular hospital in my area. The insurance company is then invoiced $10,000. I get paid about $300 of that amount, the anesthesiologist receives around $800, and the hospital gets the rest. But that same procedure can be performed just as safely and comfortably in my office—and when it is, the insurance company will probably pay only $2,500-$3,000. They save at least $7,000! Bypassing the hospital isn't just a bargain for the insurance company, however: Physicians are paid more, and patients are often more comfortable as they think of the procedure as more like an office visit and less like surgery. In short, it helps keep the overall cost of medicine down and it's a win-win-win situation: better for the insurance companies, the doctor, and the patient. It's good business and better medicine.

Because we're reimbursed at a higher rate, I'm able to run a profitable practice in which I see only twenty to twenty-five patients a day; another physician who doesn't have the negotiating power of our group may have to see forty to forty-five patients daily to stay afloat financially. I'm able to provide better care for my patients because I'm not overextended: I give full wellness exams and talk with each patient about preventive medicine. Physicians who are seeing forty-five patients a day simply don't have the time to provide this level of care.

I'm proud to say that in our office, the patient reigns supreme. Every staff member knows this and operates accordingly. We all want what's best for each and every woman who walks through our door. However, we can't afford to lose money on a patient. Medicine is, indeed, a business, and anyone who believes otherwise is sadly mistaken. We all need to make a living, and physicians are no exception: We spend years of our lives and thousands of dollars to achieve the expertise we need in order to practice medicine, and then work long, exhausting hours to ensure our patients' health. And while making piles of money isn't the primary goal of most physicians, we earn every penny we take home.

CONDOMS GONE AWOL

Patient: "We were having sex, and we lost the condom."

Me: "Okay, let's take a look."

The patient scoots down to the end of the table, puts her feet in the stirrups, and I begin my search.

Me: "I'm looking, but there's nothing there."

Patient (seeming very concerned now): "What? Oh crap! It must have gone into my uterus!"

This scenario occurs at least a couple of times a year in our office. Sometimes I find the condom stuffed all the way in the back of the vagina. Other times, it's simply not there. Where it went, I have no idea. The fact is that the vagina is like a sock. If a condom is lost in the vagina, then it's in the vagina. There's simply no place for it to go. It can't travel to your fallopian tubes or uterus. I've seen women scratch themselves raw trying to find that lost condom, while others are afraid to attempt to retrieve it.

Me: "I'm looking everywhere, but it's not here. Maybe it fell out in the sheets."

And then I provide an anatomy lesson.

HIT ME WITH YOUR BEST STUFF

Physicians do not get kickbacks from pharmaceutical or medical device manufacturing companies. There, I said it.

It seems to me there's a misconception among the general public that big pharma and medical device manufacturing companies wine and dine doctors—and even go so far as to send us on lavish vacations and deposit money in our bank accounts—so we'll prescribe their drugs or purchase their equipment. Patients have asked, "Why are you writing a prescription for that drug? Do you get something for it?" My answer is always the same. "No, we get nothing." It wouldn't be fair of me to speak for all physicians, but never once have I been approached by a representative from a company that was trying to bribe me, looking for some sort of quid pro quo. I guess I do understand where patients and the general public get the idea that physicians are lavishly wined and dined. It's definitely the stuff movies are made of. If you've seen *The Fugitive* with Harrison Ford, you know what I'm talking about. When this film was popular, several patients asked me if I attended dinners "like that." In the past, doctors were courted—there's no doubt about it. And there have been widely publicized whistle-blower lawsuits alleging improper marketing or kickbacks by pharmaceutical or medical device companies, so I guess I can understand why the general public feels the way it does.

Needless to say (but I will say it anyway), no physician should ever write a prescription or use a medical device because they received a gift from a vendor or were somehow bought off. It's unethical and illegal, and strict governmental regulations have been enacted to prevent this type of behavior: The Physician Payments Sunshine Act, which is part of the Affordable Care Act, requires manufacturers of drugs, medical devices, and biologicals that participate in U.S. federal health care programs to report certain payments and items of value given to physicians and teaching hospitals.[3] So do we get anything from these companies? Yes, we do. We're "showered" with pens, notepads, and an occasional lunch brought into the office so reps can tout their products for five or ten minutes to a captive audience while we munch on the sandwiches they brought. But let me be perfectly clear: We write prescriptions based on each patient's needs and what we think is best for that patient—not based on what company's name is on the pen we write with, or which rep brings in the best sandwiches. And those pens, notepads, and lunches we receive don't get swept under the rug. Instead, they're logged as gifts. The company that provides us—or any other physician's office—with these freebies must, by law, record this information online. In turn, the physician's office ensures everything has been recorded correctly. This data is published annually and is available to the public.

So whatever was going on twenty or thirty years ago with physicians being wined, dined, and sent on vacations by various medical companies no longer happens, and that's exactly the way it should be—and always should have been. I find it interesting, however, that our congressmen and senators, the very people who wrote the Physician Payments Sunshine Act, (which requires that I get put on a list saying I received a $1.29 pen or a pad of sticky notes from a pharmaceutical company), don't institute a law prohibiting themselves from getting their pockets lined by lobbyists. And believe me, their pockets are filled with a lot more than sticky pads.

As in every other industry, there are numerous medical conferences throughout the year. In the OBGYN arena, there are general obstetrics and gynecology conferences, plus those for ultrasound, cancer,

---

[3] American Medical Association. *Physician Financial Transparency Reports (Sunshine Act)*. Retrieved from http://www.ama-assn.org/ama/pub/advocacy/topics/sunshine-act-and-physician-financial-transparency-reports.page?

surgery, women's health, and more. The trade show associated with each conference provides an excellent opportunity for vendors to get their products in front of their potential customers. Every vendor's booth is overflowing with gifts for conference attendees: mugs, pens, sticky notes, and even the occasional beach bag. Honestly, I don't want any of that crap. Every once in a while, a vendor will be giving away a sleeve of golf balls, and I'll take those, but that's it. We have plenty of pens in my office, and I don't really want a coffee mug with the name of a drug company on it. I may be in the minority, however: There are plenty of physicians who can't seem to turn down anything that's gratis. They wander the aisles of the exhibit hall, stuffing plastic bags with all the free s*** that's offered. I have no idea what they do with all that junk, but I guess doctors are no different from so many other people who can't resist giveaways no matter how cheap or useless the items are.

Some pharmaceutical companies invite physicians to group dinners at upscale restaurants. These functions are for physicians only—spouses or guests are not allowed unless they work in your office. They always bring in a speaker to educate the doctors about a specific product. I don't relish an evening away from home and my wife—I'm away from home enough already—so I attend only two or three of these functions a year, for one of two reasons: if the product or topic is something I'm interested in or need to learn about, or if I'm invited by a drug rep who's gone the extra mile in securing free medicine for an uninsured patient, then I'll do the rep a favor and attend. And believe me, these dinners aren't lavish. It's typically a pre-set menu, and if you order a glass of wine, you pay for it yourself. The same doctors who grab all the free stuff at trade shows regularly attend these complimentary dinners. My partner and I joke about seeing the same physicians at every dinner we attend. Somehow I doubt we can chalk it up to coincidence.

I hope patients will rethink their perception that physicians receive all sorts of booty from medical company reps, and that those freebies guide our decision-making. We're hardly the only professionals bombarded by sales reps. Manufacturers try to woo decision-makers in every industry, and they use many of the same tactics. For example, educational institutions attract the attention of textbook salespersons, who bring loads of pencils, erasers—and that old standby, sticky pads—to hand out to potential customers. I can honestly say, though, if pens, paper clips, notepads, and a roast beef sandwich now and then—or an occasional dinner accompanied by a long-winded speaker—influence my choices for a patient's treatment, I shouldn't be practicing medicine. No matter the enticement, my patients' health and well-being will always be my first and foremost concern.

A DIZZYING CONCERN

It was one o'clock in the morning. As I was donning my gown and gloves, the patient was out of control—screaming her head off. Between pushes, she looked at me and said, "Two weeks ago, I was playing with my son ... you know the game where you put your head on a bat and spin around until you get dizzy. Well, I was doing that and now I am worried my baby will be born dizzy."

NO FAVORS ALLOWED

Professional courtesy, taking care of another physician and/or their family without charging, dates back to Hippocrates. But today—thanks to our government—it's illegal and considered insurance fraud.

When another professional comes to my office, I see nothing wrong with telling her, "You don't need to pay your $20.00 co-pay," or, "I'm not charging you a deductible." But I can't. As unfair as I think it might be, if I don't collect that money, I'm violating the law. I'm committing insurance fraud. And I have to do things by the book; otherwise, I risk being in huge trouble or even losing my license to practice medicine.

I may not like all the rules and regulations, but I understand that the government wants to prevent fraud. Theoretically, there are ways around the law, though: For example, a physician might bill his fellow physician the co-pay as required, and then write it off before he pays it. That's legal. The physician just has to bill his fellow physician first. I'm not recommending anyone try this, mind you. Unfortunately, our industry is so regulated, doctors are almost afraid to breathe for fear of violating some law. And heaven forbid they make a misstep where Medicare's involved—they could end up sharing a prison cell with Big Bubba or Big Bertha. Still, I think it's a shame physicians aren't allowed to give each other a break on fees from the get-go just for being part of the fraternity, so to speak. It's sort of like chef Gordon Ramsay treating chef Giada De Laurentiis to a meal at his steakhouse in Las Vegas: It's professional courtesy—and that should be okay in the medical industry just as it is in other industries.

TICK, TICK, TICK

Many years ago, a patient came in because she was concerned about a lump on her labia, the lips that surround the outside of the vagina. She'd tried to check it out on her own, but she was a large woman and couldn't contort her body to get a good view, nor did she have a partner to look for her. The patient was alarmed because the lump seemed to be growing, so she finally made an appointment to see me. As she climbed up on the exam table, I said, "Okay, let's take a look." She wasn't kidding. The lump was huge—about the size of a nickel. And it was alive. A tick had found its perfect paradise: a warm, moist, remote home with an endless buffet of blood. I numbed the area and removed the complete lump, head and all, and the entire process only took—dare I say it?—a few ticks of the clock.

WELLNESS EXAMS

Let's face it. Going to the gynecologist isn't exactly any woman's idea of a fun time. I doubt any of my patients wake up the morning of their annual exam and pop out of bed exclaiming, "Whoo-hoo! I get to see my gynecologist today! I'm so excited, I can hardly wait!" But these visits are vital to keeping women healthy for the long run.

Annual exams allow OBGYNs to spot signals that something is amiss, and alert us to issues that might warrant a closer look. For example, both uterine and cervical cancer can be prevented if they're caught early enough. We can pick up signs of cancer in its initial stages, before the cells have mutated into the full-blown disease; but if a woman doesn't come in for a checkup for a decade, she robs herself of the opportunity to catch this condition and stop it in its tracks. The same goes for many other serious diagnoses.

I've had women who haven't seen a gynecologist in eight or ten years make an appointment with me, perhaps because they're bleeding abnormally or are experiencing pain. And it turns out that the symptoms that finally drove them to my office were signs of full-fledged cervical or uterine cancer—both of which would have been much more treatable in their earlier stages. Others have had squamous-cell carcinoma on their vulva. They've been peeking at this thing for years, thinking it was just a scar or something—and risking it spreading.

But although yearly checkups can detect and prevent serious diseases like breast and cervical cancer, the number one reason I recommend that all women see their OBGYN for an annual visit has little to do with their gynecological health: It's the fact that many women don't see a family practitioner or internist for routine check-ups. About half of my patients don't. For these women, the gynecologist is the only health care provider they see on a somewhat regular basis, and if they neglect that yearly visit, they're getting absolutely no health care for years at a stretch. In essence, for many women, I'm their primary doctor.

The American Congress of Obstetricians and Gynecologists recommends that gynecologists perform full wellness exams, and I think that's wise. But this recommendation isn't always followed—far too many OB-GYNs equate "annual exam" with a Pap smear and a breast exam.

Since I'm often the only doctor a woman is seeing, it's important that I give as comprehensive an evaluation and exam as possible, to help prevent women from having issues down the road. Ideally, my patients' family doctors or internists ensure they're getting good preventive care; but unfortunately, I can't rely on my patient's primary care physicians to make sure that they're getting routine screenings like colonoscopies and bone density tests because many of them don't have primary care physicians. I'm it. So I have no problem writing orders for blood work or other tests, because I don't want to miss something. It comes down to doing what's best for my patients—and what's best for them is staying healthy. If it's possible to catch existing conditions before they get worse and prevent problems down the road, why shouldn't I? In many cases, if I don't, no one else will.

While I'm qualified to give comprehensive wellness exams and preventive care (OBGYNs who see patients in an office must answer questions on wellness exams and vaccinations on their recertification exams), I don't want to manage patients' chronic non-gynecological conditions. If a patient's cholesterol or blood sugar warrants attention, I refer her to a doctor who can better handle these issues. If a woman has hypertension (high blood pressure), heart disease or diabetes and she isn't pregnant, it's in her best interest to see a primary care physician or a specialist who's keeping up with the latest recommendations and treatments for that condition. While I'm happy to prescribe bloodwork and other tests, if there's an abnormality and it's outside the realm of my expertise, I'm going to send the patient to someone who is an expert in that area.

From Head to Toe and Down Below

Most women visit their OBGYN only once a year for their annual exam, but that one appointment can cause a great deal of anxiety. I understand. Many people aren't comfortable with the thought of removing their clothing and having their private parts inspected by a doctor. But it's necessary, so I find ways to make the appointment as simple, easy, and painless as possible while conducting a thorough exam.

Knowing what to expect when you visit your OBGYN for an annual exam can help make the appointment less stressful. In my office, a complete wellness exam begins before the patient dons a gown. If it's her first appointment with me, I take a full medical history. At every wellness visit, even if I've been her doctor for years, I'll sit down with the patient first thing and ask questions: "So what's going on this year? Are there any changes? Are there any medical issues? Any surgeries? Is there anything you're worried about?"

After the patient changes into a gown, she's ready for the physical part of the assessment—which involves much more than a mere pelvic exam. I check her from head to toe. . I listen to her heart and lungs, check her thyroid, do a breast exam, put my hands on her stomach and look at the vaginal walls and the cervix. And, of course, I do an internal exam, which includes visually examining and feeling the cervix, uterus, and ovaries, and looking for any abnormalities. If she's due for a Pap smear (more on that in a moment), the exam includes that test as well. Depending on her age, she'll also get a rectal exam during which I check for blood. In addition, if she's not in a monogamous relationship, she may get genital cultures so I can make sure she hasn't contracted any sexually transmitted diseases.

The pelvic exam is only a small part of the exam as a whole and, if treated with delicacy, most women come through it without feeling traumatized. I do several things to relax the patient and give her a sense of control: First, I choose the appropriate speculum—the right one for the job and the one that will be most comfortable for the patient. Just like there are different sizes of clothing for each body type, there are various sized specula, and selecting the proper one can impact the exam: A wider speculum is typically used on women who've had children; a smaller, shorter one is used on women who haven't given birth; and a longer speculum is needed in order to see the cervix in overweight women.

I'm pretty sure a gynecologist's office is one of the last places a woman wants to be surprised, so I never insert a speculum into a patient without touching her on the leg first and saying, "Okay, now I'm going to put the speculum in." The genitals are a sensitive area, and if you touch a patient there without any warning, she might jump off the table—or even lash out and kick you in your jewels—an involuntary reaction, of course.

I continue to tell my patient what I'm going to do next throughout the exam. "All right, you might feel a bit of cramping as I do the Pap smear." Before I remove everything, I let the patient know. "OK, we're done with that part of it." And when I'm ready to use my hands to physically examine the patient, I say, "Now, you're going to feel a touch and perhaps a bit of pressure." I try to be gentle and straightforward, and hopefully allay as much anxiety as I possibly can.

Afterward, once she's redressed, she comes back to my office for a recap. I'll tell her what I've found and we'll talk about any follow-up care or tests—for example, if she's forty or older, we'll schedule her mammogram.

Since I know that I'm serving as primary care provider for many of my patients, this recap covers more than gynecological health. I discuss any vaccinations a patient might need, and recommend screenings based on her age and risk factors. For example, when a patient turns fifty, I talk to her about scheduling a colonoscopy and seeing a gastroenterologist. If she's not regularly seeing a general practitioner,

I may be the only one keeping tabs on these important aspects of preventative care.

Pap Smears

The American Congress of Obstetrics and Gynecology recommends that women who've always had normal Paps and who don't have human papillomavirus (HPV) undergo a Pap smear every three years and an HPV screening every five years. Only women who've had an abnormal Pap smear or have other specific risk factors need to be screened more often. This recommendation isn't arbitrary. It was set by the United States Preventive Services Task Force, by people who've studied this issue extensively. They found that screening this way is both cost-effective and effective in detecting cervical cancer; but this guideline isn't always followed.

Often a patient will be surprised that she doesn't need an annual Pap smear because her former physician administered this test every year. I explain that the Pap smear we use today is not the same as the test that was used fifteen or twenty years ago. "The Pap smear in your age group screens you for human papillomavirus," I'll say. "And before your sample is analyzed, mucous and blood are removed, and it's spread out just one cell layer thick, making it much easier to spot any abnormalities. So it's very, very, very accurate. The chance of someone who's had normal Pap smears their whole life getting cervical cancer within three years is almost zero. There's no need to do that Pap smear every year if you're never had abnormal results."

So why wouldn't a doctor follow the guidelines for administering Pap smears? Perhaps he just doesn't care, or maybe he doesn't have time to explain why many women don't need a Pap every year—he simply performs the test so he doesn't have to justify why he didn't. Another possibility is that he doesn't believe the recommendations or doesn't know what they are. Or, maybe he thinks women deserve an annual Pap smear. I can understand that last argument, but by the same logic I deserve to strike it rich in the lottery.

Also, some OBGYNs believe that if they tell a patient she needs a Pap smear only every three years, she won't come back until she's due for her next test—a valid concern as many women have begun skipping annual exams in the years they don't need a Pap. While a patient does herself a disservice when she forgoes her annual exam, in many cases, it comes down to the bottom line for doctors. A patient who comes every three years doesn't bring in as much income as one who makes an appointment annually. For many physicians, it's easier to tell a woman she needs an annual Pap smear (or let her assume she does), than explain that she doesn't and then convince her that she still needs to get in the stirrups every year.

To me, it's worth it to take the extra couple of minutes during an appointment to explain why a patient still needs to come in every year regardless of whether she's due for a Pap. Yes, it takes a bit of extra effort, but it helps my patients understand that annual exams are in their best interest.

BODY ART WHERE THE SUN DOESN'T SHINE

Very few people sported tattoos when I was young. They were popular among sailors, soldiers, and so-called tough guys, but the average Joe rarely went under the needle. Of course, most women never even thought about marring their skin with permanent ink. But times have changed quite a bit, and tattoos are fairly commonplace among the women I treat today. Some of my older patients even have them—usually a small, tasteful illustration that's easily covered by sleeves or other items of clothing. Not all women's tattoos are tiny, elegant, and concealed, though. Some are gaudy and decidedly unladylike. I've seen all kinds, including several that should never be exposed to the light of day.

Red hearts on breasts are among the most popular designs I've seen. Getting a tattoo in that particular spot might have seemed like a good idea at the time, but any woman who's gotten a tattoo of any kind on her breast clearly hasn't thought about the future. Breasts, unlike wine, do not age well. In ten or twenty years, assuming there's no artificial enhancement to keep them pointing upward, those once-firm orbs are going to resemble half-filled water balloons. And as they sag, so will their artwork. Those once recognizable inked hearts will begin to look like ink blots from a Rorschach test. And since some women place their tattoos so they can be seen when they wear low-cut blouses, they shouldn't be offended when people stare at their drooping ink splotch.

Some women like to decorate their breasts or hips with spider tattoos, which is very creepy to me. I'm scared of spiders, I really am, and whenever I see a real one, I do a record-setting sprint in the opposite direction. I'm not ashamed to admit it, either. So when a woman comes in with a spider tattoo, I'm kind of freaked out. I don't run, but I do let her know how I feel about spiders just in case I start acting a bit flustered. Another tattoo I see every now and then is in the shape of a small vagina. I'm not sure what the significance is, but I don't want to know, and I don't ask.

The most memorable tattoos I've seen are ones women created for themselves that held some kind of special meaning. These patients obviously thought long and hard about what they wanted before getting inked, but for the life of me, I have no idea how they came up with the design or why they actually had it done. One of the most unusual tattoos I ever saw was just above a woman's vaginal area: an image of a penis with arms chasing a vagina. I couldn't imagine what she was thinking, so I had to ask.

"Interesting tattoo. Can you explain?" I said, expecting a profound explanation.

"Oh, you know, I don't know," she replied. "I just ... wasn't really thinking." *Yikes*. There was no philosophical reason—in fact, no reason at all—behind her "masterpiece." She just did it. *That thing is there forever,* I remember thinking. Unless, of course, she decides to have the tattoo removed by laser.

Several of my patients have a man's name tattooed on or near their genitals: "Dan's Place" or "Bill's Property" with an arrow pointing toward their private parts, or something to that effect. When I see those, I always ask, "Well, are we still with So-and-So?" If she answers in the negative, I often say, "Laser tattoo removal might be the way to go."

Not long ago, piercing seemed to replace tattoos as the new wave of body art. Multiple piercings of ears became popular as well as nose, tongue, and eyebrow piercings. Some women took things to a much lower level, though, and my nurse and I have seen our share of pierced belly buttons, labia, and clitorises. I can't even begin to imagine the pain involved in piercing such sensitive areas. During the last few years, though, we've seen less of these. I'm not sure why, but perhaps a newer fad is on the horizon. I usually don't comment on piercings of the lower body unless my patient is pregnant—in which case I recommend they remove them before they get too far along in their pregnancy. These things should not be in place when a woman goes into labor. Any woman who's pushing out a small human certainly doesn't want to add to the agony by having a piercing ripped out at the same time.

LOOSE LIPS

Patient: "Do my lips look normal?" (Hint: She's not talking about her mouth.)

Me: "Yup ... It's normal for you."

After having children, certain women come to me because they don't feel tight anymore. I suspect it's not that they themselves feel a physical difference as much as that their partner does. The labia acts sort of like a piece of elastic: when it's stretched out over and over again, as in childbirth, it eventually loses its ability to snap snugly back into place. And just as elastic loses some shape as it ages, so does the labia. As if that's not enough to make some women feel like an old pair of sweatpants, imagine what it's like when they start comparing themselves to the spreads—and I mean that in every sense of the word—of beautiful women in men's magazines. They can rationalize away the differences in terms of most physical attributes: the women in the photos are younger, they've had breast/booty enhancement or waist-reduction surgery, the pictures are Photoshopped, etc.; but as women scan the page from top to bottom, they may notice a huge difference they'd never before thought about: Those pinup models have perfect labia! Their outside lips are very, very small. And if you're among the women asking yourself (or me) why your genitals don't look like the ones in *Playboy*, the answer's simple: Most of those perfect models have had labia reduction surgery.

Believe it or not, I often get asked about this type of surgery, and sometimes it's needed, especially when a woman has extremely large labia. The American Congress of Obstetricians and Gynecologists (ACOG) outlines specific measurements and certain cases in which labia size can actually result in painful intercourse or cause discomfort when a woman wears jeans. Both are good reasons to have the labia reduced.

According to the ACOG, women should not seek labia reduction surgery for aesthetic purposes, and I agree. I try to emphasize to my patients that, unless they're having actual problems stemming from the size of their labia, they shouldn't even consider it. But there are always doctors who'll perform just about any type of surgery for a price, and labia reduction is now a booming business for some plastic surgeons. How do you tell a woman who's determined to look like a model in the latest issue of *Playboy* that a sleeker, more streamlined labia's not going to magically transform her into someone else? I do my best to point out to patients that most magazines are crammed full of pictures of beautiful men and women, both clothed and unclothed, who don't represent the norm. Most women don't weigh ninety-nine pounds and wear size zero dresses—and few normal women have perfectly shaped, photogenic labia. I get my point across to many of my patients, but labiaplasty's still a huge market, thanks to the Internet, slick marketing campaigns, and appealing advertisements.

MARKETERS AND MALPRACTICE LAWYERS

Have you ever noticed the number of law firm advertisements on TV these days? Many of them tout the services of attorneys who specialize in medical malpractice or other issues involving the medical community. Unfortunately, we Americans live in a sue-happy society, and that's bad news for this country's physicians. It's tough to practice medicine when every move you make is under a microscope, and a horde of hungry lawyers are chomping at the bit to take a huge bite out of you. OBGYNs are no exception; in fact, we might be under even more scrutiny than many other specialists because we may be blamed for problems years after the fact. Not everyone has a perfect baby, and not everyone has a happy outcome. Theoretically, parents can sue me seventeen years after I deliver a baby, when their precious darling misses the winning free throw during the state basketball championship. Maybe their child's birth was a difficult one, or maybe it was routine; it really doesn't matter because, by the time a lawyer finishes making mincemeat of that birth so long ago, I'll look like Attila the Hun. Perhaps you believe I'm exaggerating, but today's legal medical climate is so rocky, doctors have to practice defensive medicine in order to protect themselves. And that's never a good thing for doctors or their patients.

Take the morcellator, for example. This extremely valuable device was once commonly used to perform laparoscopic hysterectomies on abnormally large uteruses containing fibroids. A normal uterus is about the size of a pear, but some patients have large uteruses containing basketball-sized fibroids that can't be removed through the

small incisions used in laparoscopic surgery. In these cases, the morcellator once made a huge difference: It divided the uterus into manageable sections so it could fit, piece by piece, through a tiny opening.
It helped a lot more women than it hurt as it allowed them to avoid
the risks and recovery time of abdominal surgery.

Unfortunately, though, a small percentage of women may have
suffered prematurely because a morcellator was used to whittle
down the size of their uteruses. Unbeknownst to their doctors, these
patients had an extremely rare form of cancer called Leiomyosarco-
ma (LMS), which can form inside a benign fibroid. It occurs in approx-
imately one in one hundred thousand women, but in women who
have fibroids, LMS is more frequent—about one in every three to five
hundred. This is one of the most aggressive and deadliest forms of
cancer, and patients diagnosed with it have a poor prognosis: there's
no effective treatment. Women survive only through a stroke of
luck—if a hysterectomy is performed and a tiny uncut fibroid containing the deadly cancer is fortuitously removed, the patient may stand a
chance. More likely, though, morcellation worsens the prognosis because the tumor is sliced into smaller pieces, which can spread more
easily throughout the abdomen.

That's exactly what happened to an OBGYN who underwent a laparoscopic hysterectomy and morcellation a few years ago. The case
created a huge uproar among the medical community; though the
FDA stopped short of pulling the morcellator off the market, it cau-
tioned doctors to warn patients about the risks and suggested the instrument be reserved for use on smaller uteruses—which, of course,
made no sense because those were easily extracted through small
incisions. Hospitals stopped using the device and lawsuits cropped up
across the country; but physicians involved in the procedure weren't
the ones who were sued. No, lawyers baited their hooks for the big-
ger fish: the company that manufactured the morcellator. And the
company stopped producing it. Just like that, a beneficial medical
advance took a huge step backward. Many women who have large
uteruses no longer can opt for laparoscopic hysterectomies because
doctors no longer have access to the morcellator. In the years since

this piece of equipment was taken off the market, I've had several patients who would have benefitted from it, but they had to undergo open procedures.

I'm a big believer in setting out the options for my patients and allowing them to decide for themselves. Sure, certain choices involve some risk, but a lawyer with visions of owning a vacation retreat in the Caribbean shouldn't be the one making those decisions for them. And that's exactly what those lawyers do when they sue manufacturers for millions and millions, forcing them to stop production of some beneficial piece of equipment. Why not just caution physicians and medical centers to warn patients, "You have a medical condition, and you have choices. I'll explain each of your options, their benefits and risks. You need to carefully consider all your options. Ask me any questions you want, and I'll be honest with you. When you make your decision, we'll continue from there."

Not only are valuable tools being pulled off the market; tools are being pushed for purposes that aren't optimal. I consider one of the greatest medical marketing campaigns ever invented to be the promotion of the da Vinci robot. This tool certainly has its uses, but those applications are limited when you factor in the increased cost of a patient's care and the added length of time in surgery. In the right hands, though, the da Vinci robot can be an advantageous piece of equipment. For example, one doctor I know is able to perform eight radical prostatectomies a day on an outpatient basis using the da Vinci robot, and the patient goes home that very day. Each procedure takes about forty-five minutes, which is considerably less than the three hours doctors who don't use the device spend on each surgery. If you ask me, that's pretty amazing.

In my opinion, though, the da Vinci robot is a waste of time and money when it's used for laparoscopic hysterectomies. I've performed hundreds of them with and without this equipment, and I've found using the device slows me down and makes the patient's incisions much more uncomfortable. But the company that sells this technology is a marketing genius. The manufacturer sells each machine for

$2.4 million and plasters the media with upbeat promotions about how convenient and cost-effective the da Vinci can be for doctors and patients; and, the general public buys into those advertisements hook, line, and sinker, just as they do with the drug ads that bombard them every time they turn on the TV. When patients come to me and ask if I'll use the da Vinci when performing their surgery, I say, "You want a da Vinci hysterectomy? Sure, I'll do it, and here's what's going to happen: You're going to have four incisions instead of three, and they'll be higher on your body than the laparoscopic incisions. It's also going to take me an hour to perform the surgery instead of the normal thirty- five minutes. So do you still want me to use the robot?"

Of course, not all advertised surgical instruments or drugs are bad; but patients need to get the facts from their doctors before assuming a drug or procedure is right for them. For instance, if you need surgery, ask why a robot is or isn't being used and find out about your other options. Ask, "How will this impact the cost of my procedure and the length of time I'll spend in the hospital? How will it affect my recovery?" The same goes with pharmaceuticals: If you see an ad for a medication that seems like it would be a good fit for you, ask your physician about possible side effects and alternatives. And always get a second opinion if you're not sure if a treatment is right for you.

I don't know of a single doctor who wants his or her patient to go through more pain or pay more than is necessary, but many times, our hands are tied. Our actions often are dictated by manufacturers who inundate consumers with advertising campaigns so effective, people believe their products can perform miracles. And in a society that's quick to sue and practically allergic to taking blame, we also must be ever vigilant about lawsuits. Marketers are driven by profit, and what's profitable for pharmaceutical companies and manufacturers may not be what's best for patients. More and more, money, not the patient's welfare, dominates the medical climate. As a result, one instrument becomes widely accepted as the pinnacle of cutting edge technology while the other dies a quick death—all based on profit. How sad.

MIDNIGHT MADNESS

It was a few minutes before midnight. The phone rang.

I rolled over in bed, rubbed my eyes and answered. Not surprisingly, it was a patient. "I'm bleeding pretty heavily," she explained, her voice laced with concern.

Then she added, "You know, I have an appointment to see you at 10:30 tomorrow morning." It turns out she'd called my office several days earlier with the same complaint and had scheduled an appointment that was, at that point, merely hours away. I just about smacked my skull on the headboard. *Seriously?!*

"Well, see you at 10:30," I replied. And then I hung up.

*****

It's amazing how urgent many medical concerns become after dark. For some patients, the significance of every little twinge is magnified after midnight, and I get calls about all sorts of concerns at all hours of the day and night—from worries that something is wrong with an unborn baby to inquiries from patients who simply can't sleep.

Fielding calls from patients after hours is part of my job—it comes with the territory—and I don't mind responding to legitimate concerns no matter how late (or early) it is. But as a physician, I have a very different perspective of the definition of an emergency than most of my patients.

To me, the issue of whether to call the doctor in the middle of the night is black and white, but I've been to medical school and have years of experience in determining what constitutes an emergency. In most cases, I know almost right away if a patient needs immediate treatment when she calls. To my patients, however, this is often a very gray area. I try to be understanding of that, and I even find some of the things women call about funny—though it's not nearly so amusing in the moment, when I'm roused from sleep by my ringtone.

Pregnant patients often call me asking what medications are safe for a cold or cough or stomachache while they're expecting. I'm fine with that—to them, it's an emergency and I'm glad they want to protect their babies. But when a woman contacts me at 2:00 a.m. complaining that she's had a cold and has been coughing for three or four days, I'm not nearly as pleased. I try to be respectful, but I have to ask, "If it wasn't an emergency at 2:00 p.m. yesterday or the day before, why is it an emergency now?"

Sometimes I wonder if patients assume I just sit by the phone in my off hours awaiting their calls. I think they forget that when they contact me after hours, they're taking me away from time with my family or getting me out of bed. Women call in the early morning hours because they're getting up to go to work, or they're just getting home from working the late shift. They're already up, so they figure they may as well call about that issue that's been nagging them for the past few days. What they haven't stopped to consider is that just because they're awake doesn't mean I am, too.

Of course, there are times when I'm more than willing to be awakened—for example, when a woman's water breaks or she's in severe pain. It's because of times like this that OBGYNs are on call after hours. Responding to patients when they have truly urgent concerns is part of our job and it's essential to giving quality care.

The Gray Area That Isn't

There are plenty of reasons for calling in the middle of the night that some of my patients see as gray areas, but to me, some of them are so far from gray they may as well be fuchsia. One of my favorites is when a patient picks up the phone to let me know she's out of birth control pills.

Assuming she hasn't just returned from a year stranded on a deserted island or hasn't just lost all her possessions in a house fire, there's no reason she should wait to call me until just a few hours before she's due to take a pill she doesn't have. Still, I've gotten that call at 7:30 or 8:00 on a Saturday night, and the woman on the other end laments, "Well, I'm gonna be outta pills tomorrow." That's not an emergency—it's something she should have thought about and taken care of days before. She saw it coming. She has the pack right in front of her and can see at a glance how many pills she has left. Not to mention the fact the she probably wouldn't be in this predicament if she came to the office for a yearly exam. When women who are on oral contraceptives come in for an annual appointment, they leave with a prescription that includes enough refills to last for a year.

That's the one scenario to which I don't respond to a call after hours. I'll text my answering service. "That's not an emergency. They can come in Monday." If a patient has simply planned poorly—or failed to plan at all—I'm not going to give her a refill until my office is open.

At Midnight or in the Morning?

Though I might think it on occasion, I'm never going to ask, "What were you thinking? Why the hell did you call me at three in the morning?" I get that my patients don't always know what's considered an emergency and what's not because that's not their area of expertise.

At the same time, I try to educate my patients so they're able to decide what's worth a midnight call. At almost every visit, I tell them to go right ahead and wake me if any of the following apply. So pick up the phone at 3:00 a.m. if:

- You're pregnant and think you're in labor or your water has broken.
- You're pregnant and your baby has stopped moving.

- You're pregnant and have a fever of 101 or higher.
- You're pregnant and experiencing bleeding at least as heavy as a menstrual period.
- You're bleeding so heavily you would otherwise go to the emergency room.
- You're in severe pain—again, bad enough that you'd head to the ER—regardless of whether you're pregnant or not.

So if you're not expecting, there are only two reasons to give your gynecologist a wee-hours wake-up call: heavy bleeding and severe pain. Insomnia isn't on the list.

Then there are symptoms that shouldn't be ignored for days, but can still wait until morning. I'd love it if my patients would stop to ask themselves, "Do I have to make this call right now?" before dialing, as many times they'd be able to determine they could put their concern on hold for a few hours.

Do yourself—and your doctor—a favor and wait until daylight if:

- You're pregnant and have a cough or cold, a runny nose, an ear infection, a dental problem, diarrhea, or constipation. These things can be safely treated with over-the-counter remedies. (Our practice and many others list medications that are safe during pregnancy on our website.)
- You've been sick for three days and haven't yet called the doctor.
- You think you have a yeast infection or a bladder infection.
- You're pregnant and experiencing light spotting.

While I tell my patients that it's fine to wait until morning to call about each of these things, I totally understand if they call about spotting during pregnancy—it's not normal, and it's especially worrisome for many expectant mothers to whom nothing is inconsequential when it comes to the health of their babies. Still, when I do get that 3:00 a.m. call about spotting, I always tell my patient to call the office as soon as it opens in the morning, and to make an appointment to be seen before noon.

I never want my patients to put off calling me if they're genuinely concerned, even if I know that what they see as urgent really isn't. It boils down to this: If you think it's an emergency, don't hesitate to call. But stop to think first.

A PROBING PREDICAMENT

If I feel something out of the ordinary during an exam or a patient tells me she has abnormal bleeding, I perform an endovaginal ultrasound. For those who've never had one, this procedure involves inserting a long, thin wand into the vagina. Of course, I practice "safe" ultrasonography: I cover the probe with a condom when I use it, then toss the condom when I'm finished. That reminds me of a new patient I once had ...

My nurse escorted the woman into the exam room, asked her to change out of her street clothes, and told her I'd be in soon. Now, the room contains a trash can for regular trash and another for medical waste. Condoms from the endovaginal probe go into the medical waste bin, but for some reason or other, my nurse had forgotten to close the lid. I walked in and found my new patient staring into a trash can piled high with used condoms. She turned to me with a horrified look on her face, and I knew she was wondering what she'd gotten herself into. I remember thinking, *Oh my God! How do I explain this?* and did my best to enlighten her about how we use condoms for the endovaginal probe. I don't think she believed me for a second. I completed the exam, but to this day, she's never come back. I'm sure she thought my explanation was just a lie to cover up the truth about all the wild parties and orgies we threw every night after regular office hours.

CHOOSING A GYNECOLOGIST: LOOK BEYOND GENDER

In my town in Florida there are just a handful of female gynecologists. All of them are booked for four months solid. Me? My appointment book is filled for the next week and a half. That's fine with me—my practice is thriving—but it is telling.

Most female OBGYNs' offices are packed to the gills—all they need to do is hang up a shingle and they're almost guaranteed a busy practice because some women want to be seen by a female gynecologist. Period. They simply feel more comfortable with a female doctor examining their most private parts and have never even considered going to a male OBGYN. I can understand that. But I also understand that a doctor's gender doesn't guarantee good care.

Some of my patients had always seen female gynecologists before coming to me, and many of them are amazed that the exams I give are painless. I can't tell you how many times I've heard, "That's it? That was so easy. Why did it always hurt before?" Their past experiences had convinced them that every gynecological examination involved some degree of necessary pain, and these women seem surprised that my exam is the gentlest they've ever had. Who would have thought they'd get such treatment from a *male* OBGYN?

When a woman visits my practice, I schedule forty minutes with her; before I begin the examination, I take time to talk with her and go over her medical history. Sometimes, she'll tell me that her first appointment with her previous doctor—usually a woman—consisted of a thirty-five second exam by a physician she didn't meet until she was naked on the table. I can only infer that the female gynecologists these patients have seen in the past were rushing through the exam to get to the next patient.

I think it's every OBGYN's responsibility to respect women and treat them as gently as possible. Just because I've never been in the stirrups doesn't mean I don't understand how uncomfortable it can be, and I do all I can to make that time free of pain and surprises. Judging from what I've heard over and over from women, a lot of female gynecologists don't do that.

What qualities should patients appreciate in a physician? Characteristics such as ability, expertise, knowledge, and reputation are key. Is your gynecologist sympathetic, attentive, approachable, and accessible? These should be the qualities a woman looks for in her gynecologist, not gender.

Some of the differences between male and female gynecologists date back to the residency program. As I've mentioned, residency is an incredibly rigorous, grueling program during which future doctors work long shifts—often with very little sleep in between.

Because of the long hours and tough conditions, many residents become somewhat hardened by the end of the program. Though I'm not sure why, it seems women generally come out of residency much more cynical and less empathetic to their patients than their male counterparts.

The women who stick it out through residency and become doctors are undeniably resilient and talented, but it seems that some of them hold their own toughness over patients' heads. In the delivery room I sometimes hear, "I've had a baby, so I know you can do this without an epidural." or, "I survived years of residency, so you can make it through hours of labor."

When a patient is in pain, my default reaction isn't, "Suck it up—you'll be fine." It's "Let's see what we can do to make you more comfortable." As a man, I've obviously never experienced a baby growing and kicking inside me, but I can imagine what my patients are going through and can empathize when they're uncomfortable. The least I can do is try to make their pregnancy easier. So when my patients are in labor, I offer epidurals to alleviate the pain. I provide IV meds. In short, I try to make their labor as pleasant an experience as possible.

Women need to hear about every treatment that's available to them so they can make informed choices about their care. For example, if a patient is experiencing heavy bleeding, I lay out all her options, both surgical and nonsurgical, explaining the benefits and the downsides of each. It's up to the patient to decide which option is best for her. But, I've noticed that female gynecologists are less likely to recommend surgical procedures to their patients. In some cases, this means that patients don't even hear about all of their treatment options, and may not be getting the best care for their specific needs. Gynecologists who recommend more surgical procedures perform surgery more often; in turn, they're often more skilled in these procedures. If a male OBGYN operates more frequently than his female colleague, perhaps he has better surgical skills."

I've had women come to see me because they've been suffering from heavy bleeding for several years, and their female gynecologists gave them just one treatment option: the pill. When I talk to them about endometrial ablation (a simple in-office procedure that eliminates the lining of the uterus and can reduce menstrual bleeding), they ask, "Is this new?" I explain that it's been around for two decades. But they weren't offered this alternative. Regardless of the medical condition, I encourage patients to be involved in making decisions about their treatment.

My point isn't to bash any of my colleagues—not at all. Rather, I want to urge women to choose a gynecologist based on skills and work ethic rather than simply selecting a doctor based on his or her gender. Why does a future physician, male or female, choose the OBGYN specialty? We want to have positive interactions with our patients, be part of the miracle of birth, and make an impact on women's health and wellness; and, we're drawn to the variety of medical and surgical aspects of the specialty. It's not because the physician wants to look at vaginas all day.

Choosing a Gynecologist

So how do you choose a gynecologist if gender isn't the primary deciding factor? Unfortunately, there's no failsafe method for selecting a doctor who provides compassionate, skillful care. But there are a few ways you can narrow down your options.

Board Certification

I'd love to be able to say that if you choose a physician who is board-certified, you've done your due diligence, and can see that doctor with confidence. I can't. Of course, making sure that an OBGYN you're considering has board certification is a good first step, because it ensures that person has passed their written and oral boards and has been re-certified every six years. But on its own, that's not enough.

The recertification process primarily serves to ensure that a doctor's knowledge isn't too far below what's considered "normal" for a physician in a particular field. Every year, OBGYNs are required to read a series of articles and answer a few questions about each one—a sort of open-book quiz. A score of eighty percent or above is considered passing, and it's easy enough that essentially everyone passes. The exam that we're required to take every six years is a bit more challenging; but it's not as stringent as the original certification exam, and as long as a doctor demonstrates adequate knowledge, they'll pass. However, do you really want to choose an OBGYN with simply adequate knowledge with no guarantee that they're applying this knowledge to your care?

Board certification isn't necessarily a sign that a doctor is keeping up with the latest research, guidelines, and treatments—it just means they were able to pass a test on those things. For example, every doctor in our group of four hundred OBGYNs is board-certified—it's a requirement for membership. But only about thirty percent of these doctors follow the current recommendations regarding Pap smears.

Of course, not being board-certified should be a big red flag. The vast majority of practicing OBGYNs are, and if a doctor hasn't met that standard in this day and age, you need to ask why—or just avoid them altogether. There are plenty of board-certified OBGYNS, and no woman needs to settle for one who's not.

Read the Reviews—With a Grain of Salt

Websites like Healthgrades, Vitals, and RateMDs provide potential patients with reviews of the physicians they're considering. While you shouldn't make a decision based solely on online opinions, these websites can offer valuable clues about what a doctor is really like. If the majority of a doctor's reviews are negative, that's a warning sign—just don't put too much stock in a single review.

Keep in mind that if a doctor has only a few reviews, those reviews will likely be negative—people are much more likely to write a review when they're angry or dissatisfied. (When was the last time you wrote a review about good service?) But, if forty-something out of fifty reviews are positive, that's probably a good sign that most of that doctor's patients are happy with the care they're receiving.

Of course, being happy with care and actually getting care that's worth being happy about are two very different things. An OBGYN can have a great personality and send his patients home with a smile, but that doesn't guarantee that he's a good doctor—it's just a sign that he's well-liked.

Clues in the Office

A doctor's staff and office can tell you a lot about that physician's practice, so pay attention to the clues you can pick up before you enter an exam room. When you call to make an appointment are you treated like a valued patient, or does the person on the other line seem annoyed to be talking to you? When you arrive at the office are staff members friendly and attentive, or are they rude and dismissive? What does that say about the doctor they report to? I think the staff is a reflection of the physician. (On a side note, if you really like your doctor but haven't had a positive experience with his or her staff, let your doctor know! Even the best physician may not be aware of how a staff member is treating patients—I know I always appreciate this sort of input.)

Look at the office itself, too. Is the reception area inviting and warm? Is it clean and in good repair? An attractive office doesn't necessarily indicate that the doctor offers good care; but an office that's falling apart, disorganized, and looks like it hasn't been vacuumed in two months should set off some pretty loud alarms in your head. Online reviews and input from current patients about the sorry state of the waiting area and exam room should make you think twice: If a doctor doesn't care enough to maintain his space, what does that say about the effort he'll invest in providing quality care?

In addition, consider how long you spend in the waiting room. Is it a reasonable amount of time? Or, if you know someone who sees that doctor regularly, ask her how long she has to wait—you'll get a much more accurate answer from a patient than you will by calling the office.

Personally, I have no patience when I have to wait to see a doctor. My time is valuable, and if I show up at 12:40 p.m. for a 1:00 p.m. appointment, I expect to be seen by 1:15 p.m. or 1:20 p.m. at the latest. Yes, emergencies happen—I get that more than most people—but if I need to wait for over an hour, I'm never going back to that office. If a doctor is planning his day well, there's no reason patients should have to wait for hours on end. If you're spending ninety minutes in the waiting room before every appointment, your doctor hasn't scheduled appointments appropriately.

As I said, emergencies happen. Babies make their grand entrance without any consideration to schedules. But how does a doctor handle the times when he can't see a patient as planned? When I need to leave the office for a delivery, the patients whose appointments I'll miss are given several options: They can see my partner, see the nurse practitioner, or reschedule. And if I'm going to be late or unable to keep an appointment, my staff does its best to catch patients before they come in.

*****

I like to joke that once you see a male gynecologist you'll never go back. I'm only half kidding.

And I'm not kidding at all when I say that, in general, I've found male gynecologists to be more sensitive and more attentive to patients' needs and concerns. No, I've never had a Pap smear or been in labor. But I've performed more Pap smears than I can count and have cared for thousands of patients as they've brought children into the world, and I think that makes me worth considering as an OBGYN. (Would you discount a veterinarian because he's never had fleas or a hairball?)

CAN'T TELL MOM

According to the latest guidelines, women don't need a pelvic exam or Pap smear until they're twenty-one unless they're sexually active or experiencing problems, like abnormal bleeding. That doesn't stop some mothers from bringing their daughters in for an exam much earlier than that because they believe I can tell them whether or not their child is having sex. Well, I hate to disappoint these moms, but they need a quick refresher about doctor-patient privilege: When their daughters come in for a consultation, they become my patients—and I won't divulge anything to a mom without my patient's permission.

And how do I find out whether or not a patient is sexually active? Contrary to popular belief, a pelvic exam probably isn't going to provide the answer. Most of the time, I'd be better served staring into a crystal ball than looking at a patient's private parts. I suppose if a patient's hymen (a thin membrane that surrounds the opening of the vagina) is intact, it's reasonable to conclude she hasn't had intercourse; but if the hymen is torn, as is often the case from tampon use or merely engaging in sports or other activities as she grows up, I can't just assume she's engaged in sexual activity. A female's response to the pelvic exam might give me some indication (those who've had intercourse typically are more relaxed during the exam), but I'm never one hundred percent certain because I can't be sure a patient is telling the truth.

When a mom brings in her young daughter and insists on an exam, I do hope the girl will be honest with me, though. I usually ask the mom to leave the room before I sit down and take a history and (hopefully) develop enough rapport with the patient that I can provide advice and treatment, if needed. But I'm still not going to tell the mom a word of what her daughter says unless her daughter specifically gives me permission to do so. Not one word. Bottom line: If a female isn't having problems, sexually active, or twenty-one, she doesn't need to see a gynecologist; and, if mom insists on bringing her in anyway, she needs to remember I'm not a genie, and there are certain wishes I can't fulfill.

THE NOT-SO-AFFORDABLE CARE ACT

A lot has changed in the medical world since the Affordable Care Act (ACA, also known as Obamacare) was signed into law in 2010. Unfortunately, many of those changes have resulted in medicine that's neither affordable nor rooted in good care.

Let me qualify that by saying that the Affordable Care Act isn't without its benefits. For example, anyone can now get insurance regardless of pre-existing conditions. So a woman who has breast cancer can purchase an insurance plan for the same price as any other woman her age in her area. That's a wonderful thing. The ACA also dictates that insurance companies can't drop a patient because they get sick, and that there are no longer limits to how much an insurance company will pay in a patient's lifetime. Prior to this legislation, patients with cancer or other serious diseases would reach a lifetime maximum, a point at which the insurance company would no longer pay for their care.

As an OBGYN, I believe one of the biggest benefits of the Affordable Care Act is that insurance companies must now cover one hundred percent of the cost of preventive services such as annual wellness exams. Women can get a yearly checkup without shelling out a co-pay. The same applies for Pap smears, mammograms, bone density screenings, colonoscopies, vaccinations, and many contraceptives for patients in the recommended age ranges: All are covered in full. Most insurance companies have said that they'll continue to offer this sort of coverage for preventative care even if the ACA fails or is revoked. They recognize that, in the long run, it's a win-win for them and for patients.

Higher Costs, Narrower Networks

Despite these benefits, the Affordable Care Act clearly has issues, the biggest of which is cost. This plan simply didn't take into account the cost of medicine. You'd think the powers that be who designed the ACA would have anticipated its impact on health care expenditures, but it's clear they didn't.

From the get-go, proponents of the ACA claimed it would lower the cost of health care, but that hasn't been the case—far from it. Costs are rising exponentially and will continue to spiral upward.

Before the Affordable Care Act, elderly people normally paid substantially more for health insurance than younger individuals. Now, prices have been equalized to a great extent: the elderly and those with pre-existing conditions pay less than they did a few years ago, while those who are young and healthy pay much higher rates. As a result, more of the elderly and the sick—those who couldn't afford insurance in the past—have purchased insurance plans, while younger, healthier people have opted not to be insured because they don't think it's worth it or they can't pay for it. The penalty for not having health insurance is so low that many younger Americans—perhaps those thirty-five or even forty and under—have opted to simply pay the fine rather than shell out several hundred dollars per month for each member of their families. To them, this strategy makes financial sense, and they know that if they get really sick or are injured, they can still show up in the emergency room and receive care—insured or not. While these individuals may receive a bill, they can apply for temporary emergency Medicaid to cover it, offer to pay a reduced rate, or simply not pay at all. After all, it's not as if the hospital can "take back" the care once it's provided. So, in the minds of many who don't buy into Obamacare, health insurance just isn't necessary.

Insurance companies are being forced to offer lower-cost plans to people who need more care, and are losing the income they once generated from those who rarely met their deductibles. As a result, the cost of insurance is soaring: The rates insurance providers were charging simply weren't high enough to cover the amount they've had to spend.

While some of my previously uninsured patients were able to get coverage through the ACA when this legislation went into effect, many are now discovering that the Affordable Care Act isn't nearly as affordable as it once was. Those who shopped for health insurance plans in 2016 have found that rates are much higher than they were during the open enrollment period for the 2014 plans. So many people are back where they started, in a sinking boat with no life preserver. And scores of citizens who once had affordable health insurance have joined them: Either they can't pay the increasing health insurance premiums, or the plans they can afford are so restrictive that they don't bother purchasing insurance at all.

Insurance plans' higher price tags impact employers as well— which in turn affects employees. Many of my patients have lost the health insurance they had through their jobs because the plans their employers offered didn't meet ACA regulations. These companies were forced to switch to ACA-approved plans and have since dropped health insurance coverage from their benefits packages altogether due to the costs of the plans themselves and the sky-high deductibles that their employees had to pay.

In short, the health insurance landscape isn't promising: It's starting to crumble in many places, and I don't know what it will look like in a year or two. Insurance companies are already pulling out of the ACA marketplaces and the insurers that remain offer plans with extremely narrow networks. For patients on these plans, there simply aren't enough doctors or hospitals to go around.

This not only limits patients' selection of hospitals, specialists, and other health care providers; it limits my ability to provide recommendations based on what's best for my patients rather than on the shrinking pool of physicians in their plans' networks. For instance, what if I need to refer a patient, but the specialist I know and trust won't take her insurance? This significantly impacts patient care, and it's hard to practice medicine with your hands tied behind your back.

These narrow networks are one reason that many doctors are very selective when it comes to working with ACA insurance plans. Another is the bottom line: Many of these plans reimburse physicians at lower rates than non-ACA plans. Our group of physicians will only accept ACA plans that pay the same rate as the other plans with which we contract. Sadly, we've lost patients because we don't accept their insurance plans; others choose to pay me directly out of pocket while keeping plans we don't work with. But I never want to be in a position in which I have to consider how I'll care for a patient based on how her insurance plan will reimburse me. By only accepting certain plans, we protect ourselves from that.

While the Affordable Care Act was a beautiful idea from a social standpoint, in practice it's far less attractive. I've had very few patients tell me that the ACA was good for them.

NO FREE LUNCH

"Why can't our health care be free as it is in Canada?" I've lost count of the number of times I've heard these words, but I have some strong thoughts on the subject ...

The simple answer is that it's not free. Canadian citizens and those who live in Europe, Australia, and many other countries around the world participate in one form or another of universal health coverage, that's true. But it's not free. In fact, it's extremely costly in more ways than one.

Universal health coverage (sometimes called universal health care or UHC) aims to provide health care to all citizens of a country no matter what. Sounds ideal, doesn't it? Here in the United States, there's a broad range of political views about health care, including the opinion that it should be free. Well, there's no such thing as a free lunch, so who do you think is going to pay? YOU. That's right. You, me, and every other citizen of this country who is gainfully employed. UHC requires a lot of legislation, regulation, and taxation. Those who live in countries with UHC pay heavily for the privilege—in the form of taxes.

There are two sides to health care: the cost of the care and the *quality* of the care. Imagine going to your family physician because you have a horrible pain in your back. "We'd better do an MRI," she says. Then your name gets put on a list and you wait. A week. Four weeks. Four months. That's the way it is in Canada. (Of course, in our litigious society here in the U.S., we have the opposite: Practically everyone who walks into an emergency room gets a CT scan or an MRI. Well, perhaps that's an exaggeration, but we're certainly test-happy here in this country—because we're sue-happy. That's not good medicine either.) Not only does Canada have the most expensive UHC in the world, but it's an underperforming system. I've done many laparoscopic hysterectomies on patients from Canada: They come to the U.S. for their surgery and pay me out of pocket because in their own country, they'd have to wait a year or two. They can see me and be scheduled in a week or two. Not every country that has universal health care has an underperforming system, but for certain, in every country that offers some sort of universal health care, working citizens pay dearly.

In the United States, we have a progressive tax rate: the higher your income, the higher your tax rate. You pay a certain percentage of your income as tax, from ten percent to just under forty percent. We simply don't collect enough in taxes to fund universal health care. In some UHC countries, citizens give more than half of their income to the government! In those countries, it doesn't matter if you're a physician or a laborer, if you're a business owner or you work at McDonald's, you keep less than half of what you earn. So if you work forty hours a week and earn $1,000, you may take home only $400. The other $600 goes to the government. If you make $100,000 a year, you take home just $40,000. Are you willing to give that much of your income to Uncle Sam? That's what would happen here in the United States if some politicians got their way when it comes to UHC.

When I'm talking to a younger crowd, I hear, "Oh yeah, free college education. Free medical school. Everything free. That's the way it should be." This is the philosophy they embrace. Here's my response: "Let's assume you're in med school and the teacher says, 'Tomorrow there will be a test. Everyone in the class will receive a score of seventy. It doesn't matter how much you study, or if you study at all. Everyone gets a seventy.'" When I share this example with a college student, it gets their back up. "Wait a minute, why should the person who didn't study get a seventy and I study like crazy, get every answer right, and I get only a seventy? That's not fair."

Precisely.

So when it comes to health care, what's the answer for us here in the United States? I wish I knew. Minds far more brilliant than mine have yet to figure it out. But just remember, there's no free lunch.

YOU'VE GOT TO BE KIDDING

I started my practice as an energetic—some would say naïve—young doctor, and I always encouraged my patients to ask questions when they needed answers. "There's no such thing as a stupid question," I'd say, and I'd do my best to provide honest, accurate responses. I'm no longer as young or as naïve as I was in those early days, but I still urge my patients to ask questions, and do my best to give truthful answers. I've learned, though, that there are stupid questions. Some are just funny, or weird, or crazy, but I've heard just about every question imaginable, and many are just plain dumb. Sorry, but it's the honest-to-goodness truth.

My all-time favorite questions come from pregnant women. Here are a few that top the list:

"My friends have told me that now that I'm pregnant, I shouldn't raise my hands above my head because the umbilical cord could get wrapped around the baby's neck. Is that true?"

"I don't want to go out in the rain since I'm pregnant because it'll get the baby wet. What should I do?"

"I enjoy taking baths and swimming, but I'm afraid my water will break while I'm in the tub or pool, and I won't know. What should I do?"

"I was at the beach and got a bit of sunburn. Will my baby be sunburned, too?"

"At my last ultrasound, you told me that my baby's head was down. I've been busy walking around today. Will my baby have a headache?"

MEDICAID

We live in a great country where people who lose their jobs or become disabled can still receive health care, even if they can't pay for it. Our system supports these patients who would otherwise fall through the cracks, and I'm glad this safety net exists for their sake. But I also believe that as a general rule, people should get what they work for.

A growing number of Americans are choosing not to purchase insurance in favor of going on Medicare or Medicaid. Everyone in the U.S. who has worked throughout their lifetime becomes eligible for Medicare when they turn sixty-five. Those who have worked throughout their lifetimes and paid into the system begin getting back what they contributed in the form of health insurance, though they still are responsible for co-pays.

In contrast, Medicaid is based on income, as well as the amount of debt a person has compared to their income. For example, a young person with a relatively low income will likely qualify for temporary emergency Medicaid if they incur a $20,000 hospital bill. Medicaid is designed to serve as a safety net for people who can't afford health insurance; but this fallback form of coverage is becoming the go-to for a growing number of Americans.

Patients with Medicaid can receive health care for free or with low co-pays, though eligibility requirements and benefits vary from state to state. Unfortunately, these low (or no) costs for patients mean minimal reimbursements for doctors. Like many of the insurance plans available through the Affordable Care Act, Medicaid reimburses physicians at a very low rate—as little as a third of the rates commercial insurers pay. As a result, doctors are forced to make a hard business decision: Is seeing Medicaid patients worth their time?

Doctors don't have to accept Medicaid, and many don't. Those doctors who do choose to accept Medicaid's low reimbursements often can't afford to spend a lot of time with each patient. They have to pack more appointments into an hour so the practice ends up in the black. And this adds up to a lower quality of care for all their patients, no matter whether they have health insurance or not.

Abuse of the Safety Net

Several years ago, when we still saw patients on Medicaid in our office, one of our patients who hadn't been working got a job—one that offered health insurance. But when she showed up for her appointment the following year, she was back on Medicaid. "What happened to your health insurance?" I asked.

Without batting an eyelash, she looked at me and replied, "Well, you know, I had to pay forty bucks a week out of my paycheck. I figured out that if I go part time, I don't have to take the health insurance, and I get my Medicaid back—and my Medicaid is free. I love me my Medicaid."

WHAT? You have to be kidding, I thought to myself. And in that very instant, I made the decision to stop accepting Medicaid. Here was someone who'd made a conscious decision to work less—and therefore earn less—just so she could get Medicaid instead of purchasing her own health insurance. I have a problem with that. It isn't right. That's abuse of the system, and the system is broken. I won't care for patients who've opted to work fewer hours so they don't have to pay for health insurance and can get free Medicaid instead.

That's far from the only example—this system is rife with abuse. I've had patients who drop their health insurance coverage as soon as they learn they're expecting because in the state of Florida, pregnant women almost automatically qualify for Medicaid. That way, they avoid paying their insurance plan's deductible and get free coverage. I have a problem with that.

I also have a problem with the fact that patients who strategically surrender their insurance in favor of Medicaid are restricting the care they receive. The coverage offered by Medicaid is very limited—for example, Medicaid caps the number of pregnancy visits and ultra-sounds that a pregnant woman can have, regardless of her specific medical needs.

To be clear, I have no qualms when a pregnant patient loses her job and applies for Medicaid so she can get care for herself and her baby. I'm all for that because it's what the system was designed for. But I've got an issue when someone makes a conscious effort to drop their insurance (by quitting their job!) so they can receive Medicaid.

At a conference a year or so ago, I sat down with one of the heads of the association that administers Medicaid here in Florida and talked with her about this abuse of the system. She told me, "Yes, we know; and no, there is nothing we can do about it."

That's part of the problem: Government agencies are powerless to address this abuse or perhaps they simply don't want to do something about it. I'm not sure which is the case, but regardless, it's hurting those it was originally designed to help, and making it harder for doctors to provide good care.

I don't have a problem with a social safety net—I have a problem with people who abuse the system. Unfortunately, a growing number of people are doing just that.

LABOR AND DELIVERY

I've had the privilege of delivering nearly 5,000 babies. Think about that … *five thousand*. And twenty-seven years after my first delivery, I continue to be awed—and honored—at each and every birth. I'm a very lucky guy.

With that many deliveries under my belt, I've seen and heard everything imaginable when it comes to childbirth. Every patient has expectations about her labor. Some women are quite realistic and others honestly believe they'll have the delivery of their dreams: Labor will involve nothing more than a slight twinge in the stomach, and will only last about five minutes before the baby pops out; the family will gather round holding hands; the new mom (perfectly coiffed and made up, with a flatter stomach than she's ever had) smiles as she holds her beautiful bundle of joy for the camera. They can dream.

Thanks in large part to Dr. Google, some women want to go through labor without any pain relief (and think they can), but the reality is that most need some assistance in the form of drugs. Part of my job is to set proper expectations, which is why I tell my patients that labor is like getting your big toe hammered every five minutes for ten hours. I don't want to scare them, but I want them to be realistic: Labor can be really, really excruciating. If, by her seventh month, a patient hasn't already consulted Dr. Google and presented me with a birth plan of some sort—or at least broached the topic of labor— then I pose the question, "What's your plan for pain relief during labor?" For those who say they haven't thought about it or don't know,

I reply, "Winging it is pretty much a bad plan. We need to prepare, because if you have no plan and do nothing, I'll just use my earplugs while we're delivering your baby." As you might guess, we then have the conversation about available options, and I direct the patient to our website for further information.

And then there are those patients who say, "I want drugs."

Something for Your Pain?

When the patient is in active labor in the hospital, a pain relief plan is put into action and IV medication or an epidural (or nothing) is administered. A drug called Pitocin is widely used today, not to relieve pain—it can actually make labor more intense—but to shorten labor. "Who wouldn't want to have a shorter labor?" you might ask. (I wonder that as well.) The answer is plenty of women—because they've been counseled by Dr. Google. Pitocin is a synthetic Oxytocin, which makes women contract. On one hand, it can make contractions stronger, but on the other, it will all be over a lot sooner. My estimate is that seventy percent of all laboring patients get Pitocin at some point, so shortening the duration of pain usually wins out over scary stories on the Internet.

First-time expectant mothers often scour the Internet for information about the pros and cons of epidurals, which ease the pain of childbirth. One myth they inevitably run across is that an epidural can slow labor and cause back pain that can plague them for the rest of their lives. Not true, but that's never stopped Dr. Google from recommending that patients just grin and bear it without any medication to help take the edge off the contractions.

It's called labor for a reason: It's hard work, and many women—or men, for that matter—have never endured anything quite so painful. Contractions sometimes last eight to ten hours before the patient is completely dilated, and then she spends the next couple of hours pushing. Breathing classes, such as Lamaze, can help; but no matter what you do to alleviate the pain of the birthing process, labor is still a lot of hard work.

And that brings me back to epidurals: They're safe, they're not going to paralyze you, and they're not going to cause chronic back pain. An epidural, if given at the appropriate time during active labor, will, in fact, help your body calm down and your muscles relax, and may actually speed up labor. It won't block one hundred percent of your pain, but it will take away about ninety percent. An epidural can change an uncomfortable experience into a pleasant one—and shouldn't you be able to enjoy the process of bringing your child into the world? I always tell patients their options: they can take IV medications, participate in birthing classes, get epidurals, or do nothing. I also discuss the advantages and disadvantages of each. Ultimately, it's a decision each patient has to make for herself based (I hope) on sound research and careful planning, not bad advice and tall tales she's gotten from questionable sites on the Internet. I realize what's right for some of my patients may not be appealing to others, and I've delivered using each option. Some have prepared for delivery by taking Lamaze or other birthing classes, where they learn natural ways to cope with labor rather than getting an epidural. Others have opted to use IV medication or an epidural at the earliest appropriate moment. Still other women reject the suggestion of an epidural, yet take no actions at all to prepare themselves for childbirth. So I'm not exactly shocked when these patients ask for an epidural once they hit three centimeters and are in active labor. Of course, a few first-time mothers have such quick deliveries, they don't need medication for the pain, but they're exceptions to the rule.

Birthing Classes

When a patient and I discuss the options for pain relief during labor, I make it a point to recommend birthing classes, but not because I want her to do the Lamaze or Bradley Method of birthing. Of course, if she wants to have a natural childbirth, that's great; but I often recommend the classes offered by our local hospital. The big benefit of these classes is that patients learn what to expect—and what not to expect—during labor and delivery. Suppose you arrive at the hospital three centimeters dilated and I tell you that I'm going to finagle the baby's thingamabob and whatchamacallit. That might make you a little nervous. But if you've attended birthing classes, then you'll understand what I'm talking about and you'll be less anxious. You won't get freaked out when we use a fetal heart rate monitor because you'll know what it is and that it's the norm.

Birthing classes are important not just for the first-time mom, but for the second and third-time mom as well because every pregnancy and every labor and delivery are different. If you've had five kids, then you probably don't need to attend a class, but otherwise, I recommend it.

At the Hospital

Patients in labor are admitted to the labor unit. My preference is to admit my patients only when they are in active labor, not when they're in the early phase, or prodromal labor. When women are admitted during early labor, they end up walking around the unit for eight hours before they're truly in active labor. I don't want to be at the hospital for eight hours longer than necessary and I'm pretty sure none of my patients do either, once they understand what labor really is.

I work hard to educate each and every patient as to what point she should call us. In fact, this is something we discuss at every single visit as a patient nears full term. "If you're at full term and contracting every ten minutes, you don't need to call. When you're contracting every three minutes for at least an hour, with contractions lasting forty-five seconds each time, and it's so uncomfortable that you can't talk or breathe, then call." And when she does call, I want to hear her voice because it can reveal a lot about how advanced her labor is. I tell my patients, "Please don't have your husband call me when you think you're ready to have the baby because I won't talk to him. I'll have to be rude to him and say, 'Put your wife on the phone.'" Hearing the husband doesn't help me—if I made recommendations based on the tone of their voices, a lot of women would land in the labor unit three days early. With the thousands of deliveries I've done, ninety-nine percent of the time I can tell if a patient is truly in labor by talking with her on the phone. In twenty-seven years I've had only one patient deliver en route to the hospital, and it was her sixth pregnancy. She called and I told her to get to the hospital, but she didn't quite make it.

Delivery Is Not Your Best Moment

When a patient is pushing, she usually poops. It's normal. When you're pushing a baby out, it's not unlike the feeling of forcing out a bowel movement. In fact, poop is one sign that a woman is pushing the right way: If she's pushing out poop, she's also pushing out a baby. Years ago, enemas were administered to women in labor; fortunately, that practice was stopped a long time ago because it's invasive, and there really is no need. I realize the idea of having a bowel movement in front of the delivery team isn't a thought most women relish; but it's funny to me that women don't want to push because they're afraid something might come out. Women may be embarrassed, but this is a normal part of the birthing process and no OBGYN is worried about a patient's poop.

And speaking of poop ... I advise my patients—especially first-time moms—to think long and hard about who they want in the delivery room. Some women seem to hold glamorous visions of what their delivery will be like. I think they've watched too many medical soap operas. The truth is that labor is a long process with all your most personal stuff hanging out in the wind for a long time: Not only are you likely to poop, you'll probably also pass gas. You're uncomfortable, dripping with perspiration, and not getting in a shower anytime soon. You may have a catheter; you may pee or vomit. Do you really want your husband's father in the room?

Hubby in the Delivery Room

When we baby boomers were born, men were banned from the delivery room. They waited in a room down the hall, often with other soon-to-be-dads. They probably worried, paced, looked at their watches, and smoked cigarettes while anxiously anticipating word from a nurse that they had a new baby girl or boy. Today, dads are almost always in the delivery room and it's been this way for the last fifteen or twenty years. The husband's role can entail multiple duties, depending on the needs of his wife: wiping a sweaty brow, massaging feet, being a cheerleader. If he attended birthing classes with his wife, then he'll know what to expect; but knowing what to expect and seeing it are two different things. At the end of the day, birth is a medical procedure and it's a big mess. Blood and fluid are everywhere. In fact, it's such a mess that we have a drape, and a big bag collects all the blood and fluid so it won't end up all over the floor—or the room. Many times I've glanced over at a dad, a 220-pound strapping guy, who's as white as a ghost with sweat pouring down his face. "Are you okay?" I'll ask. "Yeah, yeah, I'm fine," is the standard reply. Unconvinced, I ask again, "Are you sure you're all right? Because if you fall over, I'm not picking you up." Then the wife will chime in, "Honey, please go sit down." At that point, the husbands sometimes admit, "Yeah, I better sit." I've had guys pass out and hit the floor, so if I see that look in their eyes, I tell them to have a seat. So do the nurses— they don't want to pick up passed-out husbands either. They'll say, "Okay you—sit down because we don't want to be picking you up."

A lot of husbands want to cut the cord when the baby is born, and I'm more than happy to accommodate them as long as everything is proceeding smoothly and there are no emergencies. We normally put the newborn on the mom's abdomen and chest, clamp the cord, give the scissors to the dad, and let him cut. But it's not always that simple. When I hand the scissors to the dad, I'll say, "Okay now, cut really hard. It's tougher than you think." It's easy for me to say because I do it all the time; I know exactly how hard to cut it and it's not a big deal. But I've seen strong, burly guys who've tried to cut through this little cord—that's only as big around as your pinkie—as many as five times before they've succeeded. These guys are a little traumatized from the entire experience; their hands are shaking; they're worried they'll hurt their child. I get it, but it still gives me a chuckle.

I Can't Do It!

At least once a week for the past fifteen years, I've heard a mom in labor say, "I can't do it." The cervix has to dilate to ten centimeters and then the mom has to push the baby out, a process that can take five minutes or three hours. It depends on the patient, the size of the baby, the mom's strength, which way the baby is facing, and the strength of the epidural. When a mom thinks she can't go another minute, I try to lighten things up a bit: If the baby has a lot of hair, I'll sometimes braid it. The mom can't see, but husbands get a kick out of it. We docs do all kinds of things to lighten the mood and help the mom concentrate on pushing instead of focusing on "I can't."

Ultimately, most women push that baby out. But when mom yells out, "I can't do it anymore!" it's sometimes followed by, "Do a C-section. Cut the baby out! I can't push a minute longer." Usually by this time I can see the baby's head and his or her grand entrance is only minutes away. But mom is physically and mentally exhausted after ten or twelve hours of labor and two or three hours of pushing. Of course we OBGYNs encourage the mom. "You can do it. I know you can. That baby is right there. We're almost there." At this stage, babies take two steps forward and one step back every time the mom pushes: Baby comes down, then goes back a little, then comes down and goes back again. My response to my patient differs depending on the hour or the day. More often than not I'll say, "Nope, you can do it. It's right there— I'm telling you—right there. We've got just a few more pushes." If I'm feeling particularly playful, however, I'll say as seriously as I can, "No, we're not going to do a C-section because the baby is right there. But it's three o'clock in the morning, and I'll tell you what: I'm going home and getting back in bed. When you start pushing again, I'll come back." Then I'll step out of the room. Usually, in less than sixty seconds, the nurse comes out to fetch me, "Come on in, she's delivering."

There are times when mom just can't push the baby out and we need to do operative deliveries. The baby's head may be turned slightly and simply won't fit, or the baby is just too big. In these cases, a C-section is performed. And we still use forceps and vacuum devices when necessary. All three of these procedures are considered operative deliveries and are done every day in hospitals across the United States and across the globe. In good hands, they are safe options providing a better outcome for the baby and the mom.

* * * * *

Even though I've been delivering babies for over a quarter century, it's still a joy every time. Being able to be a part of such a major event in the life of a family and share their excitement over a newborn may be old hat for me, but it's a wonderful experience.

A healthy baby really is a miracle. A multitude of things have to go right from conception to delivery, and there are many opportunities for these things to go wrong. Obviously, most of the time these factors fall into place and parents are able to celebrate a new life coming into the world. Part of our job as OBGYNs it to make sure that everything is happening as it should, and intervene to get things back on track when they veer off course.

I'M WHAT?

When OBGYNs are on call for the ER, we treat all gynecological emergencies, including vaginal bleeding, ruptured cysts, ectopic pregnancies, miscarriages, and other problems that require our expertise. We also cover for the labor unit: Sometimes, pregnant women with no private physician seek medical assistance in the ER for physical issues or because they're in labor. I've delivered close to five hundred babies over the years while on call for the ER. In a half-dozen of those cases, the patients insisted they had absolutely no idea they were pregnant. "There's no way you didn't know you were pregnant," I said to them. But every last one of them stuck to their guns, claimed they had no idea, and said it was a complete shock. I didn't believe them: There's no doubt in my mind that these patients knew they were pregnant long before they showed up in the ER with "stomach pain." Most were teenagers—probably in denial—and didn't want to tell their parents about their pregnancy because of possible repercussions. Their fear trumped logic, and they were able to hide their pregnancy either because they were grossly overweight, or because they didn't show much and were able to hide their bellies with baggy clothes.

One would think that, if a woman goes to the ER complaining of pain in the abdominal area, the ER physician would see the patient and assess her—put their hands on her belly where she has pain and say, "Aha. You're pregnant." But in each of these cases, that's not what happened. Perhaps it was a ridiculously busy night in the ER, and when the patient complained of abdominal pain, she was sent off for an ultrasound or CT scan. (Abdominal pain can be associated with appendicitis, gallbladder problems, and kidney stones among other things.) The ER doctor never even touched the patient in pain. In every case, it was the technician doing the test who discovered these patients were pregnant. Imagine the tech's surprise when looking for gallstones or some other problem. "Wait a second. What's that in your stomach?" And "that" turns out to be a baby, and the "stomach pains" are labor pains. In each of these cases, the calls I've received in the middle of the night were from the technicians, who said something like, "I'm doing an ultrasound on this woman. They thought she had gallstones, but I think she's in labor." It amuses me every time.

I remember one case I covered in the ER. The woman was in her mid-forties and was morbidly obese. She tipped the scales at almost four hundred pounds; as a result, she suffered from multiple medical conditions and took several medications. When I told her she was pregnant, she was floored. The patient had just assumed the pain was caused by stomach issues, not a baby. She'd never considered the possibility she might be pregnant. She told me she'd had intercourse only one time in the past year, and I absolutely believed her. Once reality sank in, she was concerned that the medications she'd been taking would harm the baby, but I'm pleased to report she gave birth to a heathy child. I love a happy ending.

That was the only time I bought a patient's claim that she didn't know she was expecting. But when a one hundred twenty-five pound eighteen-year-old insists she had no idea there was a baby inside her basketball-sized belly, I just can't buy it.

NOT THE TIME FOR A FAMILY GET-TOGETHER

Most women come to their gynecologist appointment unaccompanied, but some—five to ten percent—seem to think it's a perfect place for a family outing. It's a bit easier for me to understand when a patient brings her spouse or partner with her, especially when she's pregnant, but loading up the kids in the car and hauling them to a gynecologic appointment is just weird. It certainly shouldn't be considered quality time, especially if mom drags them into the exam room. Young children are energetic. They want to play. They don't want to be cooped up in a small room with a bunch of instruments they're not allowed to touch. And when they're acting like kids while I'm trying to examine mom, it makes an uncomfortable exam even more uncomfortable.

So my advice: If you have to bring the kids and they're old enough to sit on their own, make them stay in the waiting room; if they're too young to be alone in the waiting room, leave the kids at home and hire a babysitter. Or, if they're in school, make your appointment during school hours so you don't have to worry about where they are and what they're doing. They'll thank you, and so will I. If you want to spend quality time with your children, that's great. Take them to a movie or to the park—but not to your gynecologist. I realize it's not always possible to leave the kids at home, but bringing them with you to your appointment should be your last option. That goes for husbands and significant others, too, unless they plan to stay in the waiting room during your visit. It never ceases to amaze me when I walk into the exam room and find my patient's spouse or boyfriend sitting in the chair at the head of the table, eager to observe. Most are very naïve about what goes on during an exam, but they find out soon enough—and I can tell you exactly what they're thinking: *What the hell am I doing here?* Their faces turn all shades of red as they observe their wife/girlfriend having her breasts examined by a strange man who then sits between her legs and does more things to her down there. Mystery solved, and most men probably consider it TMI—too much information.

I often wonder if the patient asked her husband/boyfriend to accompany her into the exam room or if it was the man's idea. I'd say it's a very uncomfortable experience for about ninety percent of the men, and I do my best to put them at ease by making light of the situation. After the exam, I often turn to the man and say, "Okay, come on up here so I can do your prostate exam." Most get a kick out of my joke, and at least they leave the exam room smiling after suffering through an awkward experience. I have to say, though, that these men are quick learners: Very few return to the exam room a second time.

Of course, it's a bit different when a patient is pregnant. She may want her husband or boyfriend with her during the exam and, no matter how he feels about being in the exam room, he pretty much needs to do as she's asked. After all, he's part of the reason why she's at this appointment in the first place. Often, when I do an ultrasound or tell them how much she's dilated, the couple is excited by this news and they focus more on the baby than the exam. That's a good thing because the exam usually is more comfortable for all concerned. Sometimes, instead of the expectant father, a pregnant patient has a female friend or her mother accompany her. I realize it's a female bonding thing, but I sometimes wonder: *Why? What's the thinking behind that? She's twenty-five and perfectly capable of being here on her own.* I've never been asked to accompany a male friend to his proctologist appointment. But if having someone there makes my patient more comfortable, I'm all for it.

TALK TO YOUR DOC—ABOUT SEX

As I've mentioned earlier, many women visit their gynecologist on a regular or yearly basis, but they may have little or no contact with any other type of physician. That's why I include general wellness checks and try to establish a positive, trusting connection with each patient. It's important that women feel they're able to open up to me and discuss their sex lives and any aspect of their sexuality in an open and nonjudgmental atmosphere. I'm here to answer their questions and guide them whenever necessary, and my job is to make sure my patients understand they can come to me about any concern without feeling embarrassed. I think it's great when they do, and I'm certainly not mortified discussing their sex lives with them or answering questions. Sex is a normal part of life. It shouldn't be a taboo subject, but many women are uncomfortable bringing it up, even when they're speaking with a trained medical professional. Yes, some women have managed to break through those barriers, but it's literally taken centuries to get this far.

My patients always manage to amaze me, and that's especially true when it comes to discovering which patients unabashedly ask questions and discuss their sex lives with me. I've had patients who appear prim, proper, and very ladylike, but they're not afraid to be blunt and use plain terms to describe their sexual activities. Bravo! I love it when the patient I'd least expect to discuss any sexual matter with me blurts out, "I can't come (or climax or orgasm)." I'm so happy to hear them open up, I typically say, "It's great you're telling me this. We need to talk about it."

But for every woman who's willing to speak freely about sex, there are plenty of patients who'd rather be confined eternally in a barn full of flatulent cows than talk about the "S" word with me or anyone else. So I ask questions and try to draw them out: "How is your sex life? How is your libido? How are things at home?" I'm not nosy or pushy; these, along with many other questions I ask at their annual wellness exam, are necessary to assess their overall health. And helping a patient attain better sexuality and enjoy a good sex life most certainly will improve her well-being. Health isn't a point on a line, but one big circle connecting every aspect of a patient's physical and emotional wellness, and I want to make sure that circle's hale and hearty.

It can be tough to get some of my patients to open up about their sex lives. I hear a lot of women say, "Oh, I don't want to talk about that." I can't force them to express their concerns, of course; but when they do bring up questions, they're often ones I've heard before—and I let them know their concerns are normal. I think the most common falsity women seem to believe is that sex is a one-sided activity—meant to satisfy the man. In other words, as long as he's having a good time, she should be okay with what's happening between the sheets—even if she isn't achieving orgasm, isn't enjoying it, and feels somewhat cheated out of pleasure. When I hear that, I can't help but shake my head and tell my patient that sex isn't just about the man. She's not supposed to give, give, give while he takes, takes, takes. If she's with someone she loves or wants to be with, sex should be enjoyable for both partners, not just the guy.

Another frustration involves the difference between how men and women approach sex. Some males do seem to have a "wham, bam, thank-you, ma'am" mentality because they're hardwired much more simply than females. I like to compare men and women to computers. When it comes to sex, men have one switch, similar to the on/off switch. The switch flips on, and then the switch flips off. And it turns on and off with barely a touch. That's why, out of the blue, a man can roll over in bed and say, "Let's have sex," then roll back over as soon as he's satisfied and snore like a freight train the rest of the night.

Women, on the other hand, are much more complex. You can flip that on switch all you want, but unless all the other knobs and dials are properly set, the screen's barely going to flicker. In general, a woman's just not going to have an enjoyable sexual experience unless some bells and whistles are added. Women need foreplay. Women need all the emotional sensations that accompany sex. Women need to be romanced. And if it's not "happening" for them, they need to let their spouses or boyfriends know.

Many of my patients say, "I have no sexual desire. I have no libido."

And I'll respond, "Tell me what's happening when you have sex."

"Well, he gets into bed and wants to have sex. So we have sex, and that's it," they tell me.

After I explain the differences between how men and women are hardwired, I always encourage my patients to sit down and have a conversation with their partner. They should be honest and reassuring, and say, "This doesn't work for me. I still love you and want to have sex with you. I want to be engaged with you, but we need to make it good for both of us … How do we do that?" Sometimes, merely scheduling a date night does the trick. Other patients tell me long "make-out" sessions—like the ones they used to have when they were younger—have created the much-needed spark.

Of course, just as some women are uncomfortable talking to their physicians about their intimate lives, many women are afraid to broach the subject with their partners. That can be a real problem, and it shouldn't be. It tickles me when a woman comes to me with a question, and it was her husband who encouraged her to ask. At least I know they're communicating about their sexual lives.

Although women can enjoy sex throughout their adult years, sometimes factors other than lack of communication intervene. Some women experience a change in libido when they go through menopause, and their OBGYN can help. If discussions and changing the way sexual intercourse is approached doesn't make things better, I usually prescribe testosterone. When women go through the change of life, they not only lose estrogen, they lose testosterone—and sometimes small amounts of this hormone can increase their libido. I've prescribed testosterone therapy for many patients, and when they return for their follow-up visit, most say, "We're happy as clams. Now everything's great."

Other conditions can also take the pleasure out of intercourse. Vaginal dryness, whether it's age-related or caused by another problem, can affect a woman's comfort level during sex, but that can be another easy fix if she discusses it with her doctor. Some women tell me they just flat-out don't enjoy intercourse because it's painful, and when I examine them, I find they have a retroverted, or tilted, uterus. Another simple solution. I tell them to experiment a bit with positions until they find one that's comfortable for them.

I've also had women tell me they don't enjoy intercourse, but they know if they fake orgasm, their partner will come. I always wonder how many of these women watched *When Harry Met Sally* to get the technique down before I say, "Well now, you should be enjoying sex, and if not, let's figure out what the problem is. Are you with the wrong partner or is there some other reason?"

One woman said she faked orgasm because her husband always felt he had to bring her to orgasm before he came. If she didn't come first, he'd just hold back and keep going and going and going, just like the Energizer Bunny, until she was desperate to get him to stop. I have to admit, that does sound tedious and unsexy as anything—one person monopolizing all the fun while the other tolerates his actions until she can stand no more. I imagine it's how I'd feel if I were invited to the home of some very distant acquaintances, and they showed home movies for three straight hours.

Actually, I think readers will be surprised to learn that the average male doesn't have the staying power many people believe they do. According to multiple studies conducted in the United States, a man typically lasts four or five minutes at most during intercourse. Don't be fooled by the guys in porno movies who last thirty minutes or more at a time. Those seemingly endless gymnastics aren't always the real deal, thanks to the magic of editing; and if some porno stars can actually last that long, well, they're not average males, are they? Remember, I'm talking what's normal. If you don't believe me, pull out a stop watch and time it for yourself.

Obviously, there are those men who fall somewhat short of the norm, but they needn't worry unless they're ejaculating in less than sixty to ninety seconds. If so, they're experiencing premature ejaculation, and some steps can be taken to help them. If a woman tells me this is indeed the problem, I ask if her husband would be willing to become part of the discussion. But in general, premature ejaculation isn't a common problem.

The women I worry about the most are the ones who've been married for twenty or twenty-five years who say, "We don't have sex anymore." When I ask them why not, sometimes they say the partner has a medical problem, which is understandable; but others tell me their husband just isn't interested. Whoa! Red Flag! Remember what I said about how men are hardwired? Trust me when I say that most men are interested. Barring a medical problem, if a guy's not interested, it's probably because he's got something going on the side. Of course, it's not my place to blurt that out, but I try to encourage my patient to discuss the problem with him, to find out why he's no longer interested, and what they can do as a couple to start connecting again sexually.

I approach the topic of sex differently with each woman depending on several factors, including age, frequency of sexual activity, sexual orientation, and the types of sexual activity she engages in. A woman's sexual orientation isn't a matter of concern to me except when it comes to the issues we discuss. I don't judge one way or the other, and as far as I'm concerned, neither does any other OBGYN. It's important for me to know, though, so I can direct patient care more accurately. For example, if my patient is a lesbian, I don't need to waste her time talking about oral contraceptives or birth control options. But a discussion about safe sexual practices among same-sex partners is relevant and worth the time.

I've also had patients who tell me they engage in anal sex, and that's perfectly fine and acceptable if that's what they and their partners like. It's my job to ensure these women know they can transmit bacteria to the vagina when they go from anal intercourse to vaginal intercourse, and to let them know they can take some simple steps to ensure this doesn't happen. That's why it's so important that women open up to their physicians and just as important that doctors ask the right questions. Every woman lives a unique life, and she has a right to enjoy it fully in every way—including sexually. As doctors, we need to equip each patient with the right information and means to make that happen.

Maintaining a healthy sex life sometimes takes a bit of work, and as long as patients are willing to discuss their concerns with their OB-GYN, include their partner in the conversation, and are open and honest with themselves, improvements can be made. Sex should be fun and mutually fulfilling. I'm not saying couples should start swinging from chandeliers, wear erotic costumes, or role play ... but then again, why not? Whatever rocks your boat.

WHAT GOES IN ...

In the course of examining patients, I've dealt with odors that would make even people with cast-iron stomachs gag. We're talking about times when I've wished I had a hazmat suit on because the stench was so strong. And believe it or not, that horribly foul odor is caused by a patient's failure to remove a small tube of tightly wound fabric used to absorb her menstrual flow. About once or twice a year, a patient calls my office and says, "I think I put a tampon in, and I can't get it out." Or, forgetting she's left a tampon in, she says, "I've had this discharge and odor for a couple of days. I've never seen or smelled anything so bad."

Believe me, neither have I. My staff encourages the patient to come in, and about half the time, I find a retained tampon. It happens to a lot of women—in fact, every woman has probably dealt with a retained tampon at some point in her life. When it happens, yes, it's smelly and sometimes difficult to retrieve—but it's not the end of the world. Nor does it result in Toxic Shock Syndrome—that happens only in extremely rare cases. I can tell you it's not a good idea to leave a tampon in for an extended period of time, though. Do you know that saying about houseguests and fish smelling after a few days? Well, you can add retained tampons to that list. A restaurant dumpster that hasn't been emptied for a week smells better than a tampon that's been trapped in your body for a couple of days. And unfortunately, that smell isn't always confined to the nether region, but can fill a whole room—which can definitely put a crimp in your social life.

Speaking of filling a whole room with the odor, we actually have a protocol in our office for removing retained tampons and bagging them up right away so the smell doesn't spread throughout the halls and into other areas of the building. Whenever a woman walks in and says, "I'm not sure what this odor is, but I think I left a tampon in. I can't feel it, and if there's one there, I can't get it out," my staff springs into action. My nurse ushers the patient into an exam room, whips out a plastic bag, and waits as I pull the offending tampon out of the patient's vagina. Then, quicker than a flash, it's placed in that bag and sealed tighter than a time capsule. The patient might be embarrassed because, admittedly, the stench is overwhelming, but again, it's just one of those things that happen in life. I can't emphasize enough, though, how important it is to see a gynecologist as soon as possible; the longer you wait, the more it can affect your well-being. You should also be prepared for a smell like no other. As I said, you won't be the first—or last—patient who's had this problem.

NEVER JUDGE A BOOK ...

"How many sexual partners have you had in your life?" That's a question I ask every patient, particularly on her very first exam. The more sexual partners a woman's had, the more at risk she is for contracting Human Papillomavirus (HPV), the most common sexually transmitted infection in the United States. It's somewhat entertaining when a new patient comes to the office with her spouse or partner: I can tell both parties are uncomfortable when I ask the question, and I wonder if the patient will tell the truth. I often make a joke out of it, look the patient in the eye, and say, "Well, you brought them in." Or, "Do you want them to leave?" Sometimes I look directly at the partner and say, "Put your fingers in your ears." Or, "I'm going to ask you next, so are you sure you want to hear the answer?"

All kidding aside, it's important to ask the question and receive an honest answer as it helps me properly manage the patient's care: If a patient is at risk for HPV, I may recommend an annual Pap smear plus HPV testing. We have patients on Medicare, which covers a Pap smear only once every two years—unless they're in a high risk category, which includes having had abnormal pap smears in the past, having had more than seven sexual partners, or having had HPV.

I've received all sorts of responses when I ask a woman how many sexual partners she's had, but the most common answer is somewhere between five and eight. A few years ago, I was interviewing a new patient and posed the question. She mulled it over for a few seconds and responded, "Well, probably around five hundred." I managed to maintain my composure and thought to myself: *She's either very popular or a nymphomaniac.* In my best serious doctor manner, I followed up. "That seems like a significant amount. Would you like to elaborate?" She matter-of-factly told me she earned her living as a prostitute. Like most people, when I hear the word prostitute, I envision scantily-clad women who walk the streets on the seedy side of town, looking to turn tricks. I must admit I was a bit shocked by my patient's response: Just when I think I've heard it all, especially after more than twenty years as an OBGYN, a new patient comes in and catches me off guard. After all, I live safe and snug in a commuter town and though I know prostitutes exist in all corners of the globe, I would have bet my bottom dollar we didn't have any in our community. We're not Las Vegas. For me, though, this patient shed new light on the oldest profession. She didn't seem to be the type to stroll down Main Street trolling for tricks and servicing twenty johns a day. No, she was well-spoken and elegant, and I assumed she was a "high-end" lady of the night.

My job is to protect the health and well-being of my patient, so our discussion moved on to how this woman protects herself from acquiring sexually transmitted diseases (STDs), and from possibly being harmed when she meets a new client in a hotel room. She said she requires condoms for every encounter, and we discussed the fact that condoms are not foolproof. No matter how cautious a woman can be, she can still end up pregnant or acquire an STD when her partner uses a condom. She asked for STD testing and, of course, I was happy to write an order. She was a bright woman and seemed open to conversation, so I asked her if prostitution was something she wanted to be doing—or *had* to be doing. Without hesitation, she declared that she was quite comfortable with her profession and that it was her way of life. Then she revealed a few details: She advertises online, sees two or three clients each week, and earns over $150,000 annually. I had no idea how an upper-echelon gentleman's companion operates her business and was amazed she made so much money. We had an engaging, enlightening conversation, and I was utterly fascinated. But the best part about our chat was that my patient was open and honest, which allowed us to have a serious discussion about protecting her health and well-being.

Since that time, I've had a few other patients who are prostitutes: Two stated straight away how they earn their livelihood and requested STD testing. I'm certain I've had other patients who engage in the same occupation but choose not to reveal it to me. Of course, it's up to the patient whether or not to divulge such personal information, but I wish they would all be straightforward for two reasons: I can then have the appropriate health discussion with them, and I may even be able to assist them in another way as I did one patient who confessed she hated being a prostitute. She was a single mom who felt she had no other options. I connected her with a local social services office and, in turn, they helped her find a new job. I was happy for her, and felt rewarded by the fact I'd been able to help a woman break the bonds of a profession she despised. I was glad to provide a small bit of guidance that ultimately enabled her move on to a brighter, more productive situation.

It's not every day I get to provide treatment for—or converse with—a prostitute, and I've discovered that those who've visited my office for treatment have interesting and unique opinions, lives, and approaches to their health. Even though they're engaging in activities that are usually associated with the shadier side of society and their profession is rarely the topic of cocktail party pleasantries, I certainly have no right to criticize them for their lifestyle. I'm their OBGYN, not their conscience; and I'm pleased when they seek my medical assistance and guidance. But if there's one thing I've learned from these particular ladies' fascinating stories, it's to never judge a book by its cover.

ASK ME ANYTHING

Most people don't actively seek an OBGYN to fill the extra seat at formal dinners, so the majority of folks we encounter are patients. There are over 30,000 gynecologists in the United States, which may seem like a lot, but that means you have less than a one percent chance of meeting one of us in a social situation. And as a male OBGYN, I'm part of a dwindling breed. According to the American Congress of Obstetricians and Gynecologists, seventy-nine percent of all practicing OBGYNs were male in 1991. By 2003, that number had dropped to sixty-one percent;[4] and in 2014, a mere twenty percent of residents training to become OBGYNs were men.[5]

Though I can't speak for my fellow professionals, I can assure you that once you get to know me, you'll find I'm actually quite approachable, I don't bite, and I don't mind answering your questions. Interestingly, I'm asked the same questions over and over again.

What's the coolest thing you've ever experienced as an OBGYN?

I've had several really memorable experiences, but I'd have to say the first baby I delivered myself is number one on my list. That was

---

[4] American College of Obstetricians and Gynecologists. (2004). *Profile of Ob-Gyn Practice*. Retrieved from http://www.acog.org/~/media/Departments/Practice/ProfileofOb-gynPractice1991-2003.pdf?dmc=1&ts=20140814T0929418526

[5] American Congress of Obstetricians and Gynecologists. (2014). *2013 Socioeconomic Survey of ACOG Fellows*. Retrieved from https://www.acog.org/-/media/Departments/Practice-Management-and-Managed-Care/2013SocioeconomicSurvey.pdf

just an incredible experience. I have to admit that some deliveries are better than others, and some are great because the families are so nice—but that very first delivery was just so cool! I also remember the excitement and utter awe I felt when I first started doing laparoscopic hysterectomies. The act of removing a large uterus, maybe the size of a football, through three small incisions was mind-boggling. The instrumentation was remarkable, but I was also proud I'd mastered a procedure that many of my colleagues didn't have the training or equipment to perform. I liked the feeling of success.

What's the weirdest thing you've ever seen?

During my training, a patient in active labor came in to the hospital. She'd had no prenatal care. The woman went on to deliver by cesarean section because the baby was breech. Unfortunately, the infant was born with a condition called harlequin-type ichthyosis, an abnormality in which the baby's skin resembles snakeskin. It's shocking to see and might have been diagnosed before birth had the patient undergone prenatal care.

What's the worst part of your job?

There's no question that the worst part of my work is when a pregnant patient is full term, and her baby—still inside her—has died. This happens in only one in 160 deliveries,[6] and usually for unknown reasons. Most times, the patient suspects that something has gone very wrong, but there is no way to sugarcoat this news. It's incredibly difficult to tell a patient who has carried a baby inside her for nine months that her child is no longer alive. Right below this on the list of the worst parts of my job is the death of a mom. It's happened twice: once to my own patient and the other time to a patient who'd been admitted to the ER when I was the OBGYN on call. The feeling of losing a patient is indescribable.

---

[6] The American Congress of Obstetricians and Gynecologists. (2009, February 20). *ACOG Issues New Guidelines on Managing Stillbirths.* Retrieved from http://www.acog.org/About-ACOG/News-Room/News-Releases/2009/ACOG-Issues-New-Guidelines-on-Managing-Stillbirths

Being the bearer of bad news is also high on the list. I wish I only had good news to offer my patients, but that's not always the case. For example, it's difficult to tell a patient she has cancer. It's a challenge to find the right words—if there are such things—and it's definitely among the worst parts of my job. Also difficult and sadly frequent is when a young couple comes in because they are newly pregnant, and I have to dash their dreams. They're so excited and full of expectations, and I wish I could affirm their reason to celebrate; but when I do an early pregnancy ultrasound and see no fetal heartbeat, I'm faced with having to tell them they've miscarried. More than one-third of all pregnancies end in miscarriage, which is more common than most people realize—not that this information makes it any easier for the grieving couple to bear their loss. I do what I can, though, to let my patients know that nothing they did caused the miscarriage: Most miscarriages result from genetic abnormalities, and are Mother Nature's way of correcting the problem. Also, I tell them about my own personal experience. My wife's first pregnancy ended in an early miscarriage, but we now have two wonderful, healthy boys.

Do you ever have to "fire" a patient?

Unfortunately, yes, and more than you'd think. I've fired patients for various reasons, including their noncompliance with recommended follow-up tests or labs. For instance, if a patient has an abnormal Pap smear, she may need a procedure called a colposcopy to more closely examine the abnormal cells taken from her cervix. If we reach out to that patient three or four times, and she doesn't schedule this important evaluation, I have no alternative but to send a certified letter explaining the issue and giving her a certain amount of time to comply (usually thirty days). If she doesn't, the letter states, she'll be discharged from the practice. I've also fired pregnant patients who refuse to undergo routine mandatory screening. We don't order these tests to make money, but to ensure we do everything necessary to deliver a healthy baby. I'm saddened when a patient puts her health or the health of her child in jeopardy because she neglects to undergo recommended testing, but I'm not distressed when I have to fire a patient for being disruptive or rude to my office staff. Any patient who screams or curses at my employees will be fired right away. My staff is always courteous and friendly and treats each patient with respect and, in turn, I expect my patients to treat them the same way.

Are You Ever Physically Attracted to a Patient?

I know some women are leery of male gynecologists because they're afraid that a male doctor might molest them, or at least that he might be turned on when he sees them sans clothing. Let me put your fears to rest. The examination I and other male OBGYNs perform is strictly clinical. Seeing and touching a woman's body in that context isn't sexually arousing to us in the least. My patient might be the most alluring woman in the world, but what's on my mind in the exam room is giving her the best possible medical care. I'm not tempted in the least. And a female assistant is with me while I perform the pelvic exam.

The funny thing is, I can examine a woman and not notice a thing about her appearance that doesn't relate to her physical well-being; but just ten minutes later, I'll see that same woman leaving my office—fully clothed—and think: *Wow, she's really attractive!*

What's it like to do surgery or cut someone open?

I remember the very first time I held a knife, preparing to make an incision. That was scary! I recall every detail of the first few surgeries I performed, all the thinking, concentrating, and worrying. But after years of performing the same procedures over and over, the actions become second nature. Surgery is part of my job as an OBGYN: I do it all the time. Of course, I'm always careful and make sure that collateral organs don't get injured, but now I no longer worry obsessively about making a mistake. No matter how many times I perform surgery, though, each procedure is always as fulfilling as the first I ever performed. I feel immediately gratified that I've helped a patient experience less pain and discomfort, but the scary part—the apprehension I once felt as a "newbie"—has disappeared.

What's your view on abortion?

First, let me say that I don't do abortions. However, I am pro-choice. I believe women should have the right to choose, though I don't like the idea of abortion being used as birth control. Abortions are common. They happen all the time—every day all over the country—and probably more than they should. Making abortions illegal wouldn't stop them, but would definitely make them less safe.

What's it like to look at vaginas all day?

It's just part of the job, and that's all it is. Believe me. An accountant would tell you the same thing if you asked him what it's like to look at tax returns all day. We're no different, really. I doubt an accountant goes to work each morning and says, "Oh boy, I get to go through a dozen more tax returns today." And I certainly don't turn to my assistant and say, "I'm looking forward to all the vaginas I'll see today." I'm a physician, not a voyeur. And I have a job to perform. When I do an exam, I'm trying to be thorough as well as quick and gentle. I look for abnormalities, and ask the patient questions that may clue me in to any problems they may have. It's entirely clinical. As I said, it's my job.

Is it okay to fake my orgasm in order to help my partner finish sooner?

Do whatever works best for you, whatever rocks—or in this case doesn't rock—your boat. If speed is your top priority, get to that finish line as quickly as you want—but keep in mind that old tale about the tortoise and the hare. Who ultimately achieved satisfaction and won the race?

Do you have favorite patients?

Let me emphasize that my goal is to make sure every patient leaves feeling like she's my favorite patient. That's just good business practice and an important key to success. Obviously, you have to provide excellent medical care, but if the patient leaves believing that I think she's special, then that's a great thing. She's happy, she'll refer friends, and she'll be a patient of mine forever. To get to the heart of the question, though, my answer is yes, I do have favorite patients. There are some I just bond with more than others, usually as a result of some difficult medical experience they've had. The effort I spend trying to help them through the event and the increased empathy I feel for what they're going through often result in stronger ties. I think back to a couple of emergency caesarian sections I performed early in my career. I still keep in touch with one of those patients regularly, via email, Facebook, and even the occasional telephone call. She became a special patient because of a unique situation. Some patients and I simply have hit it off because we have similar interests, whether it's work, hobbies, or favorite sports teams. I always look forward to seeing them. Perhaps my very favorites, though, are the ones who are always nice and appreciative, no matter what they're going through. I guess when it comes right down to it, I have a lot of favorite patients!

Do women really tell you their secrets?

Yes, although some women won't, even if the information could affect their health. Then there are the women at the opposite end of the spectrum, like the prostitutes I mentioned in the previous chapter, who are quite open and willing to discuss everything with me. I've found that many women just need to talk to a professional, and as long as they feel reassured I'm not going to judge them, they'll tell me secrets regarding their sexual relations or about affairs they or their spouses have had.

What's the craziest story a patient has told you?

I think the woman whose husband pocket dialed her while he was having sex with another woman is probably the craziest story, but the first time a woman told me she was a prostitute and matter-of-factly described the world of online prostitution … well, that was pretty crazy, too.

What's the best part of your job?

Without question, the best part of my job is the relationships I develop with many patients. Though going to the gynecologist can be a chore or an anxiety-provoking event, many women bond with me over time. I'd probably be going too far if I said they enjoy their yearly visits, but by the same token, many seem happy to see me. In fact, some patients appear to relish telling me about their year, discussing their health, and chatting about family issues. My favorite part of these yearly visits is when I see them physically relax and smile when I walk into the room. After many years, these patients are like old friends, and I'm glad my presence puts them at ease. Another great part of my job—a close second to the doctor-patient bond that develops over time—is when I deliver a baby for a family that's so excited, they burst into tears when their newborn arrives. Those deliveries do seem really special and are a wonderful part of my job.

ACKNOWLEDGMENTS

I deeply appreciate all who've help me make my vision of writing a book a reality.

I am deeply grateful to the physicians, educators and mentors who have set high standards and encouraged and guided me to meet those standards and excel during my medical training.

Thank you to the physicians and peers, and my practice partner for the positive interactions during the course of my medial career. I value your knowledge and friendship.

To B.D., a fellow resident, thank you for fueling my determination to make my dream a reality through your excitement about this book's potential many years ago

To V.T., I appreciate your encouragement and practical advice. Thank you for reading my book, commenting, and enriching my ideas.

Patients don't care how much you know until they know how much you care. And I have been blessed with thousands of patients who have confidence in me to provide them with warm, compassionate care.

My heartfelt gratitude to my wife, sons, and family. This book is only possible because of your constant love, support, patience, and strength throughout the years.

CONNECT WITH THE DOCTOR

Interested in more insight from the other side of the stirrups? Have a question you've always wanted to ask? Please visit

www.ConfessionsOfAMaleGynecologist.com

Made in the USA
Monee, IL
28 January 2025

11148077R00081